God's Tomorrow

DAVID BROWN

God's Tomorrow

SCM PRESS LTD

Unless otherwise stated, biblical quotations are from
the New English Bible

334 00590 6
First published 1977
by SCM Press Ltd
56 Bloomsbury Street, London WC1

© David Brown 1977

Filmset in 'Monophoto' Ehrhardt 10 on 11 pt by
Richard Clay (The Chaucer Press), Ltd, Bungay, Suffolk
and printed in Great Britain by
Fletcher & Son Ltd, Norwich

Contents

Foreword

Have Christians anything to say about tomorrow; about the world's tomorrow which is close at hand and which brings such great opportunities and dangers with it? Tomorrow, like today, belongs to God, and to seek his kingdom in them both is the work of mission.

I have written this book to explain what I mean by talking about mission in this way. I have had in mind many of my friends, loyal and thoughtful members of Christian congregations, who really do try to live Christian lives, but who find it difficult to associate the gospel with the secular world in which they live the greater part of their lives. I want them to see God's mission as it is now going on in the world of the newspaper headlines, in the subject matter of TV documentaries, and in the streets and public places of their own communities.

In particular, I want to share with them three convictions:

that mission is God's total activity in the world and that the church is privileged to share in it because he calls its members to do so:

that mission is concerned with the everyday life of the whole human community, its problems and opportunities:

that mission looks forward to what God will bring to pass on his tomorrow.

I am grateful to Mrs Joan Simpson for the care and attention with which she has typed two manuscript drafts of this book. Above all, I thank my fellow Christians in the diocese of Guildford who have often responded so kindly to my exposition of the themes in this book. None has helped me more than Mary, my wife, who has heard me preach and talk more often than anyone else and yet has never failed to encourage me.

David Brown

1 The Ascent of Man

The living stream

I have taken the title of this chapter from the television series by Dr Bronowski, *The Ascent of Man*. Viewers were introduced, in the successive episodes, to those who have made important contributions to the Ascent of Man. These included famous scientists of our own day, the chemists, engineers and thinkers of recent centuries and, in addition, the unknown heroes of prehistoric days who made possible the evolution and survival of *homo sapiens*. We owe them a great debt of gratitude, just as we do the thinkers and craftsmen of another TV series, Kenneth Clark's *Civilization*.

The principal heroes of these two series were mainly great names known to European history and literature. Alongside them we must put those other pioneers who at different times contributed to the progress and growth of human communities in Africa and Asia. They also made it possible for people to build great civilizations and to develop coherent and inspiring systems of philosophy and education. The fruit of their labours has been displayed in some of the public exhibitions presented in London during the last few years: the Tutankhamun exhibition of 1973, which displayed treasures from the tomb of an Egyptian king who lived in the fourteenth century BC; the Chinese Art Exhibition of 1975; the gold treasures of Thrace shown in 1976; and exhibitions associated with the World Festival of Islam, 1976. The skills which produced these beautiful things were the fruit of painstaking and careful work over many centuries, and of the courage which many individuals showed in experimenting with new materials and techniques.

The wonder and grandeur of this complex story of human development is slowly becoming part of our common heritage. Television documentaries and the weekend supplements make us familiar with the main features of many cultures which are not our own. In school, children are introduced to them in imaginative and skilful ways. In public libraries, shelves of books introduce us to the history of the ancient Greeks, or of Egypt in the days of the Pharaohs, or of mediaeval China or India, or of Africa as explorers knew it, as well as to life in these countries as it is today. We know also that there are unanswered riddles in the great carvings of Easter Island, and mystery in the mountain temples of the Incas and Aztecs of South America.

These great civilizations, as well as our own, have only flourished because at more remote times in the past other unknown pioneers opened up new paths for their contemporaries to walk in. We who live in the twentieth century AD are in debt to the pioneers who first made clearings in the forest to house their families, or planted and harvested the first meagre crops of grain: to those who first tamed dog, camel, or cow, or who gathered a band of kinsfolk into a settled village for mutual protection. We who come late upon the scene of human history stand on the shoulders of many generations.

Before the great kaleidoscope of human history, however, stretch the long ages of pre-history, during which life on our planet evolved to become the complicated and interdependent ecological system which it is today. Human beings like ourselves have been in existence for only a fragment of the period during which there have been living creatures on the earth, and all of us are the products of growth and development which took place during millions of years within the processes of evolution. It is our privilege to be, in the words of Sir Alister Hardy, 'part of a vast living stream flowing through time'.[1] To be aware of this privilege is to be filled both with awe and joy – with awe at the majesty of the complex processes which have given us life, and with joy at the privilege of being heirs to so great an inheritance. I cannot even imagine the generations of living creatures whose lives have made it possible for my heart to beat so regularly, and my body to be so stable and so efficient a natural organism.

The creativity of the Spirit

Thoughtful people have always discerned within the complex development of the natural world the influence of an inherent purpose directing and shaping the processes of evolution to particular ends. The Hebrew writer whose great poem of creation is now the opening chapter of the Bible put it this way: 'the earth was without form and void, with darkness over the face of the abyss, and the spirit of God hovering over the surface of the waters' (Gen. 1.2 NEBm). He glimpsed, within the natural universe of which he knew so little, the activity of the Spirit of God, moulding the world to God's purposes and conforming the natural universe to his will. With the greater knowledge of the processes of evolution which science has given to us we can identify more exactly than he could significant periods of creativity such as the establishment of our solar system, the beginnings of plant and animal life, and the emergence of consciousness in animals. Above all, because of its significance for ourselves, we salute the development of *homo sapiens* from other manlike creatures some thirty thousand years ago.

Many different spiritual insights and discoveries have illuminated the Ascent of Man. In Asia, for example, human life has been enriched and beautified by the teaching of Gautama Buddha and the doctrines which are associated with him. Through them people have learned to master themselves and to walk the path of moderation and self-control. They have learned also to weigh carefully the consequences of their actions, and to value humility and non-violence. Within the Islamic areas, the influence of the practice of daily prayer which Muhammad taught was obligatory upon adult Muslims has been very important. 'Like a stream of sweet water', he said, 'it flows past the door of every Muslim – five times a day they bathe in it and are clean.' The practice of this prayer has had great influence on the development of Islamic states and communities: it has produced a climate of humanity and moderation, and stimulated education and scholarship. In the Western world, the search for truth which inspired the ancient Greeks produced words and ideas which thinkers have used all through the centuries to express their growing understanding of the world. These instances are but three examples of the many different contributions which the Spirit's activity has made to human progress.

It is a characteristic of evolutionary progress, and so also of the ascent of man, that growth is made in leaps and jumps, and not in a straight line. The history of a single nation shows this, and a history teacher at school takes care to emphasize the particular periods in which a nation's history went in a new direction or some new development took place. In English history, for example, we place special emphasis upon Alfred's achievement in uniting the small princedoms into one kingdom, and upon the invasion of Duke William which brought England into living touch with European history. On the longer scale of natural evolution, there is a similar

3

emphasis upon the periods when some organisms took great leaps forward into new types of biological life, even though the leaps had been quietly in preparation for long ages before.

Teilhard de Chardin, in *The Phenomenon of Man*, pointed out the suddenness with which such changes happen and his words help us to understand the possible significance of our own age.

> Beginnings have an irritating but essential fragility, and one that should be taken to heart by all who occupy themselves with history.
>
> It is the same *in every domain*: when anything really new begins to germinate around us, we cannot distinguish it – for the very good reason that it could only be recognised in the light of what it is going to be. Yet, if, when it has reached full growth, we look back to find its starting point, we only find that the starting point itself is now hidden from our view, destroyed or forgotten. Close as they are to us, where are the first Greeks and Romans? Where are the first shuttles, chariots or hearth-stones? And where, even after the shortest lapse of time, are the first motor-cars, aeroplanes or cinemas? In biology, in civilisation, in linguistics, as in all things, time, like a draughtsman with an eraser, rubs out every weak line in the drawing of life.[2]

The average Englishman in Alfred's day would have been very surprised if he had been told that the Prince of Wessex was establishing a kingdom which would eventually become the centre of the commonwealth: such an idea would have been beyond his imagination.

This may explain why there is so much dispute about the significance of the times in which we live. On the one hand there are those who say that our times are basically no different from those of our forefathers, while, on the other hand, there are those who say that we live in a time of crisis when mankind is about to take a great new leap forward. It is difficult for the ordinary person to judge between these two attitudes, but, if Teilhard was right, that is not unexpected. If the present is a turning-point in the development of human society it is not surprising that many people do not notice it. The butterfly appears a chrysalis until the very moment when the skin is broken and the butterfly appears fully developed.

Birth-pangs of a new age

What are the characteristics of our age which make some people think that it heralds some new and dramatic leap forward in the Ascent of Man?

1. First, *the development of science and technology* which have made

our age one of change and mobility. It is difficult to measure the tremendous strides which have recently been made in scientific discovery but perhaps the point is made by the frequently repeated statement that 90% of all the scientists who have ever lived in the history of the world live and work in 1977. Each of us will be aware of this development in a particular way – it comes home to me when I recall that my physics text-book at school expounded the electronic structure of matter in an appendix which had been added after the book's first publication.

One result of this growth in scientific knowledge is the greatly increased mobility we enjoy both in travel and communications. Steamships, trains, cars and aeroplanes, have all in turn made it possible for people to move more and more quickly from one place to another, without having to rely upon beasts of burden, or winds and ocean currents. Even more swiftly, news and views can now cross national and cultural boundaries and become immediately available to anyone who possesses a radio or television.

Mobility brings change and in our times changes come thick and fast. They affect our environment, the shape of our cities, and the character of our towns and villages. They affect the way we live and our relationships with our neighbours. At a deeper level, they affect the structure of our society, its differentials and power structures, as well as the line-up of the nations and the patterns of world trade. As an example of change in our own environment we may reflect on the speed with which we have progressed from radio to television – to BBC2 – to colour television – to transistor sets – to stereo and hi-fi equipment – to video tapes – each new development comes on the market more quickly than its predecessors and renders them obsolescent.

These changes occur in the highly developed nations of Europe and the West with greater intensity than elsewhere, but they are not confined to them. Transistors are everywhere and the pop-culture of the young is a world-wide phenomenon. The explosion in scientific knowledge affects every country where there are universities or technical colleges and that is almost every single country in the world, however small.

2. A second characteristic of our age is *the increased control over natural resources which technology makes possible*. Basically, technology is linked with progress in scientific knowledge but its results are different because they are primarily practical. Technology makes it possible for human beings to make better use of natural resources so

5

that our homes become more comfortable and adaptable, and labour becomes less onerous.

Associated with technology are the words 'development' and 'pollution'. In earlier times, the lives of human people were governed by the environments in which they lived, and by the limits which nature imposed on human activity. Modern technology, however, has given mankind much greater power to organize his environment and to win a limited freedom from such natural controls as disease, isolation and climate. This freedom, however, depends upon the organization of society in a comprehensive and wide-ranging way. To take an example: it is only possible to separate people's dwellings from their places of work and to overcome the difficulties of distance if towns have one-way traffic systems to cope with traffic, and railways have sophisticated signalling and strict timetables. Both these systems, however, impose tight controls and restraints upon individuals and they affect the amenities and security of people's circumstances and their homes.

'Development' is a word with many meanings, and includes, for example, building projects in the centres of cities as well as the rapid growth of industry in some countries of the Third World. In all these areas human beings are still learning how to guide development in such a way that it improves the quality of life instead of harming it. In this learning process harmful mistakes have been and still are being made, and it might justly be said that the quality of our social engineering has failed to keep pace with our technological progress. Humanity has not yet learnt to use technological know-how with prudence and moderation. We and our contemporaries make ever-increasing use of our ability to exploit primary resources like oil, minerals and water which nature has brought into being through millions of years of evolution, but we are in grave danger of squandering this accumulated wealth within a few generations. Moreover, we use them so carelessly that we are guilty of polluting the environment with waste materials and harmful by-products.

3. A third characteristic of our age is *the necessity of interdependence between the nations*, which is itself a result of the increased mobility and development of communications mentioned earlier. The world has become one neighbourhood in which news and viewpoints are freely shared between one household and another. It is quite practicable for one man to speak to the whole world, and when an Apollo and Soyuz are linked in space, the whole human community can eavesdrop on the conversations of the astronauts. Millions have ring-

side seats through television at the Olympic Games, or the World Cup.

But interdependence has a harsher side to it. Before the war, for example, we stocked up with coal for the winter and then, provided we had been able to buy enough, had little anxiety about our heating. Today, however, many different factors affect the heating of our homes. Smokeless zones prevent us having open fires, strikes in the mines, or power stations, or on the railways mean that we are cut off from electricity supplies, and the manipulation of oil prices for political reasons makes us lower the thermostats in the central heating. It is even truer today than when John Donne wrote his sermon that 'no man is an island': we are all interdependent and therefore vulnerable to the action of others. This interdependence is not limited to relationships within individual communities but it is a fact of life for the nations across the world. This was fully illustrated in the oil crisis of 1974, when the OPEC countries suddenly raised the price of oil: if the immediate crisis is over, the longer term problems, raised by the shifts in economic power, have as yet found no real answer. They increasingly threaten the stability of the world's monetary system. More fundamental problems of interdependence arise in connection with the proper sharing of resources and the effects of pollution on a world scale.

4. Another characteristic of our age is that *people are exposed to pressures of all kinds*, many of which are far too complex for individual persons or groups to cope with on their own. It was for good reason that John Poulton chose *People under Pressure*[3] as the title for his study of twentieth-century urban living. These pressures take many forms and the following are just a few of them.

Modern communications make it possible for us in our own sitting-rooms to be spectators of events in distant places. As television viewers, we are compelled to feel anxiety about many problems for which we have no personal responsibility nor expert knowledge. We are made aware of the world problems of hunger and pollution, and feel that we are called to make some response. Yet our own personal contributions appear almost valueless, and we feel unable to do anything to resolve them.

In our highly mobile world, communities are no longer homogeneous, professing one religion and sharing a common culture. In the immigrant areas of Europe, in many urban areas across the world, in universities, in multi-national companies and international aid programmes, we meet as colleagues with people of other faiths, and different cultures. We have all to face the possibility that the beliefs of our own particular community may not be the final answer to fundamental questions about the world and human existence. The development of multi-racial communities in British and European cities has raised many urgent questions in the field of education, and community relations.

Economic pressures force more and more people to crowd into the cities where old patterns of life break down and it is difficult to achieve true community. At the turn of the century, there were only eleven cities with more than a million inhabitants, while today there are more than ten times that number and twenty of them have more than five million people living in them. This process shows no signs of abating and it is taking place, in varying degrees, all over the world. The sociological strains and stresses which this urbanization produces for many millions of people are enormous, and often they are too great for urban authorities to cope with.

The advance of medical technology presents individuals with new moral problems which they are often ill-equipped to answer. The use of contraceptives and the public recognition of abortion have made sexual morals an urgent problem for many people, especially the young. At the other end of life, physical deterioration prolonged by drugs, with consequent indignities and the threat of euthanasia, raises different but equally serious moral questions.

Finally there is the threat of racial violence on a wide scale because of the growing in-balance between the more affluent nations of the West and those of the Third World. The picture even here is not so simple as some make it out to be, for there are nations within the Third World, like Nigeria and Iran, which have ample supplies of monetary resources alongside their own internal problems of poverty and deprivation. Not all the states of the Third World are on speaking terms with one another, and many nations in the so-called affluent sector are hard pressed financially. But the in-balance is serious and sooner or later may erupt into confrontation and violence, especially if provoked by famine on a massive scale. In the background lies the continuing conflict between Russia and the Western nations, and more generally between the communist and the capitalist ideologies. This conflict is not represented just by a line drawn down frontiers in eastern Europe – it is a confrontation which takes place in many ways, and within many communities all across the world. It is a battle of ideas which takes place particularly in many uncommitted nations of the Third World where Russia or

China contributes economic aid and educational opportunities. Associated with this conflict is the threat of nuclear war.

Mobility and change: development and pollution: interdependence and risk: pressure and tension: these are characteristics of our age. Are they signs that the human story is moving into a dark period of conflict and of chaos? Or are they the birth-pangs of a new age in which mankind will take a leap forward into a new stage of development? The human community possesses greatly increased powers to control and develop the natural environment in which its members live. Will these powers be used co-operatively to enrich the whole community or will they become the means by which one group dominates and exploits another? We need a dream and a vision to inspire us all, and we shall look at this in the next chapter. Meanwhile, we shall do well to ponder words which U Thant wrote in 1969 when he was Secretary-General of the United Nations:

> Without wishing to exaggerate, I can only conclude from the information in my possession that the members of the United Nations Organization have barely ten years left in which to forget their ancient quarrels and to join together to end the arms race, to save the environment, to halt the population explosion and to provide the necessary stimulus to the development of the underprivileged countries. Unless we achieve such agreement within this next decade, I am afraid the problems which I have mentioned will have grown to such proportions that they will have become quite insoluble.[4]

The personal dimension

It is easy to express these problems and pressures in a generalized, cold way as if they were topics for a debating society. In real terms, they represent the pains and perplexities of many millions of ordinary people who were created to be God's children and who have as much right to freedom and fulfilment as any of the most favoured people belonging to the affluent sections of the human family.

The problems of the great sprawling urban areas, for example, are not simply matters for the agendas of city councils. Hidden behind these 'agenda matters' are the personal case-histories of millions of individual persons who have to cope, day by day, with their own personal problems of homelessness, of unemployment, of degrading poverty or of inadequacy. Sometimes these personal problems are documented in films like *Cathy Come Home*, or *Gale is Dead*, or in articles which appear in journals like *The New Internationalist*. More often they are undocumented and unnoticed. The anonymous subjects of these stories of human misery rarely make the headlines.

G. Butz describes in *Communion*, the Taizé Community quarterly, how he sees the black and Puerto Rican neighbourhood of Philadelphia, USA, a community filled with tired and discouraged people.

> For many years now they have accepted the inhuman conditions in which they are forced to live. For most of them the situation is so overwhelming that they are not able to see beyond it. Each day the struggle for survival continues. The present city housing shortage enables landlords to demand high rates for rat-infested, broken-down houses. Living is crowded and tensions easily explode. Young teenagers, unable to find employment, band together in gangs to express their manhood. Violence is a way of life, and the poor are forced to steal, rape, and kill one another to release their frustrations. There is little respect for human life. Fear reigns in the hearts of all, for no one is safe. Authentic human relationships are eaten away by mistrust, betrayal, and exploitation. Good teachers are rare in the inner-city schools, and inadequate training keeps 80% of the neighbourhood unemployed. They are totally dependent on their monthly government welfare check for survival. Rising food costs and large families make balanced foods a near impossibility. Health care is inaccessible. Many, unable to obtain relief from their physical suffering, turn to alcohol or drugs for consolation and relief.[5]

This is a picture which could be told time and again of deprived communities all across the world.

This book will be mainly about general problems and the responsibilities of communities rather than of individuals. I have included this section, however, as a reminder that the most general discussion is, in the end, about the problems of individual men and women, their personal pains and joys. No disciple of our Lord can ever disregard his teaching, in the parable of the Good Samaritan, that the neighbour whom we are to love is the person whom we meet on the road of everyday. Nor can we forget that, in the parable of the sheep and the goats, he identified himself with those who actually are hungry, or cold, or in prison. It is always tempting to escape from this personal dimension into a discussion of general principles. I find it all too easy a temptation to fall into, and I expect that many of my readers do as well.

2 We Have a Dream

The importance of hope

It is a human characteristic to look forward in hope: 'among the two million or more species now living on earth, man is the only one who experiences the ultimate concern. Man needs a faith, a hope, and a purpose to live by and to give meaning and dignity to his existence.'[1] So wrote a distinguished biologist, Theodosius Dobzhansky.

The previous chapter closed on a sombre note with a warning from U Thant. But this is not the only attitude which people have adopted towards the future. The science fiction writers, for example, face the future with hope and, in doing so, entertain us with their fantasies of what life might be like a hundred or more years from now. Among the most interesting is Arthur Clarke, whose paperback *Profiles of the Future*[2] is confidently optimistic. In his dream world, hover-cars make road maintenance unnecessary, instant communication across the globe removes the cost and fatigue of travel, robot freighters bring raw materials from the moon and human people have access to inventions of every kind. His boundless optimism about the ways in which human life will go on being improved and adapted to the enormous changes which will occur in the stars of our galaxy is expressed in the last chapter of his book which he entitles 'The Long Twilight'. He concludes: 'Our galaxy is now in the brief springtime of its life ... The strange beings who have adapted (to the changes in our galaxy) ... will have time enough in those endless aeons, to attempt all things, and to gather all knowledge. They will not be like gods, because no gods imagined by our minds have ever possessed the powers they will command. But for all that, they may envy us, basking in the bright afterglow of Creation; for we knew the universe when it was young'.[3] His words are a strange echo of what Sir James Jeans, the great astronomer, wrote a generation earlier: 'We are living at the very beginning of time. We have come into being in the fresh glory of the dawn. Our descendants of far-off ages, looking down this long vista of time, from the other end, will see our present age as the misty morning of the world's history.'

It is easy to dismiss such dreams as these. They appear to ignore the political and economic realities of our world, and they take no account of the fact that the majority of human people have as yet little share in the benefits which technological advance confers on a favoured minority of the world's peoples. A mammoth revolution in the world's economic system would be needed to realize even a fraction of Arthur Clarke's dreams about the future. The fact that a man can imagine such a world, however, is an indication of the possibilities which modern science has put within our grasp.

The science fiction writers are not the only ones who dream about the future. Indeed it is often those who have suffered most because of the harsh realities of our contemporary societies who continue to hope against hope. Dr Martin Luther King suffered much in seeking human rights for the negroes of America and he gave his life in doing so, but he was sustained by a great hope. He expressed this hope in his speech at the Lincoln Memorial at the conclusion of the 1963 March on Washington for Jobs and Freedom: 'I have a dream. I have a dream – that the sons of former slaves and the sons of former slave owners will be able to sit at the table of brotherhood.' He shared his dream with a wider audience in Oslo when he received the Nobel Prize in November 1964:

I conclude that this award is profound recognition that nonviolence is the answer to the crucial political and moral question of our time – the need for man to overcome oppression and violence . . . The tortuous road which has led from Montgomery, Alabama, to Oslo bears witness to this truth. I refuse to accept the cynical notion that nation after nation must spiral down a militaristic stairway into the hall of thermonuclear destruction. I believe that unarmed truth and unconditional love will have the final word in reality.[4]

Dr Martin Luther King expressed his hope in more positive terms still in the last great chapter, entitled 'The World House', of his book *Chaos or Community*.

Every nation must now develop an overriding loyalty to mankind as a whole in order to preserve the best in their individual societies. This call for a world-wide fellowship that lifts neighbourliness beyond one's tribe, race, class and nation is in reality a call for an all-embracing and unconditional love for all men. This often misunderstood and misinterpreted concept has now become an absolute necessity for the survival of man.[5]

More than ever before we need dreams to inspire and to lead us. Like Dr Martin Luther King, all of us need a dream of what life might be like, a glimpse of what it is possible to achieve and to build, a vision of what is the ultimate destiny of our race.

First, we need this vision because our perspectives are changing so quickly. We are beginning to come to terms with the antiquity of the stream of life of which we human people are part, and the vastness of the universe in which we live. We need a vision which enables us to grasp the far future in terms which have meaning for our own personal lives, and those of our families.

Secondly, we need this vision because our relationships are changing so quickly. We live in a global-village where our neighbours are not just those who live in the same street or on the same level of an apartment block. We are neighbours to the whole world. We need a vision which helps us to see these new relationships as opportunities instead of as threats.

Thirdly, we need this vision because of changes in our relationship with the natural universe. Human beings have gained new abilities and skills which have greatly extended their control over their environments. At the same time, they have increased opportunities to misuse and exploit the resources of nature, and their own minds and bodies as well. With these new powers has come a feeling of independence which depreciates wonder, discipline and gratitude. We need a vision which will enable us to use these new powers properly and responsibly.

Mankind at the turning point

Whatever vision we gain of the future to guide us through this present phase of change and development, it must be a vision which takes the whole world into account. Dr Martin Luther King spoke quite deliberately of the 'world house'. Developments in communication have made the world 'one global village', to use a current phrase, and interdependence has made its harmony a goal which all mankind must seek.

Today as never before in its history mankind is aware of itself as a family of brothers, often hostile brothers but none the less inescapably brothers rather than strangers or foreigners. From now on there is a basis in reality for the great biblical . . . statements about the one inhabited earth, about peace as the goal of justice and justice as the basis of peace, about the equal dignity of all human beings, the corollary of which is that contempt for any human being on the ground of his or her sex, race, class, religion or culture is utterly unjustifiable.[6]

'The Age of Nations is past', wrote Teilhard de Chardin. 'The task before us now, if we would not perish, is to build the earth.'[7]

The latest publication of the influential group of economists and business men known as the Club of Rome, *Mankind at the Turning Point*, underlines the urgency with which the dream of world-community must be realized if mankind is to avoid catastrophe and find a new level of well-being. It is a sequel to the first Club of Rome book, *The Limits to Growth*,[9] which was published in 1972. This earlier report was criticized on a number of important points, and in particular for its failure to recognize important differentiations within the world scene. It did, however, sharpen the debate about resources and gave warning that the resources which are necessary for the survival of human life as we now know it are limited and must be used with care.

Mankind at the Turning Point builds up a more sophisticated model of the world economy than that used in its predecessor by dividing the world into ten different but interdependent regions. It is on the whole a more hopeful book, but its writers give similar warnings concerning the dangers which confront the world community. Their analysis of future world food supplies, population growth, the trend towards urbanization, the scarcity of resources, may well be criticized in specific details by experts in these fields, but their general thesis appears sound. It is in close agreement with the warning given by U Thant which was quoted before. They express their conclusions as follows:

Suddenly – virtually overnight when measured on an historical scale – mankind finds itself confronted by a multitude of unprecedented crises: the population crisis, the environmental crisis, the world food crisis, the energy crisis, the raw material crisis, to name just a few. New crises appear while the old ones linger on with the effects spreading to every corner of the Earth until they appear in point of fact as global, worldwide, crises. Attempts at solving any one of these in isolation have proven to be temporary and at the expense of others . . . Real solutions are apparently interdependent; collectively, the whole multitude of crises appears to constitute a single global crisis-syndrome of world development . . . Mankind, therefore, appears to be at a turning point: to continue on the old road – that is, to follow the traditional route, unchallenged, into the future – or to start on a new path. In the search for such a new direction the old premises must be re-evaluated ...

In the past the world community was merely a collection of fundamentally independent parts. Under such conditions each of the parts could grow – for better or worse – as it pleased. In the new conditions ... the world community has been transformed into a world system, i.e. a collection of functionally interdependent parts. Each part – whether a region or a group of nations – has its own contribution to make to the organic development of mankind: resources, technology, economic potential, culture, etc. In such a system the growth of any one part depends on the growth or non-growth of others ...

Mankind is at a turning point in its history: to continue along the path of cancerous undifferentiated growth or to start on the path of organic growth.

The transition from the present undifferentiated and unbalanced world growth to organic growth will lead to the creation of a new mankind. Such a transition would represent a dawn, not a doom, a beginning, not the end. Will mankind have the wisdom and will-power to evolve a sound strategy to achieve that transition? [10]

The new Jerusalem

In the last section we referred to the plea which a group of economists and business men, the Club of Rome, has made for a new concept of world community leading to 'the creation of a new mankind'. I find some parallels to it in the vision of the new Jerusalem which John gives us in the book of Revelation, chapters 21–22. It comes at the end of a book which is full of puzzles and in which apocalyptic visions succeed one another with bewildering rapidity, but the outline of this closing vision is clear. It is expressed in the following verses:

I saw the holy city, new Jerusalem, coming down out of heaven from God, made ready like a bride adorned for her husband. I heard a loud voice proclaiming from the throne: 'Now at last God has his dwelling among men! He will dwell among them and they shall be his people, and God himself will be with them. He will wipe every tear from their eyes: there shall be an end to death, and to mourning and crying and pain; for the old order has passed away!' Then he who sat on the throne said, 'Behold! I am making all things new!' ... And the city had no need of sun or moon to shine upon it; for the glory of God gave it light, and its lamp was the Lamb (i.e. the Lord Christ). By its light shall the nations walk, and the kings of the earth shall bring into it all their splendour. The gates of the city shall never be shut by day – and there will be no night. The wealth and splendour of the nations shall be brought into it; but nothing unclean shall enter, nor anyone whose ways are false or foul, but only those who are inscribed in the Lamb's roll of the living. Then he showed me the river of the water of life, sparkling like crystal, flowing from the throne of God and of the Lamb down the middle of the city's street. On either side of the river stood a tree of life, which yields twelve crops of fruit, one for each month of the year; the leaves of the trees serve for the healing of the nations (Rev. 21.1–5; 21.23–22.2).

Although written nearly nineteen centuries ago, this vision expresses a concern for world community similar to that which we discussed in the previous section. Its main themes are as follows.

1. *John's vision is of a city*: 'I saw the holy city, new Jerusalem.' Contemporary cities create problems for their administrators and their inhabitants and few take pride in what we have allowed our inner cities to become or in the pollution and traffic chaos which disfigure urban life. But John lived in a country, Asia Minor, which had many rich and beautiful cities, though small by our standards. Moreover in ancient times, the city was the place where civilization flourished. Sheltering behind its surrounding walls, the city was the place where police and soldiers kept peace, where governors administered justice, where shops supplied people's material needs and provided luxuries, and where the services of doctors, lawyers and scholars were available.

2. *John's city is a human city*: When, in John's vision, the angel measured the city he used human measurements to do so. 'Its wall was one hundred and forty four cubits high', that is, by human measurements, which the angel was using (21.15–17). John saw that God's purposes are related to the human race which is the crown of his creation, and to the fulfilment of their hopes.

3. *John's city is an open city drawing its wealth from all the nations*: 'By its light shall the nations walk, and the kings of the earth shall bring into it all their splendour. The gates of the city shall never be shut by day – and there will be no night. The wealth and splendour of the nations shall be brought into it.' Merchandise and trade from every quarter of the Roman Empire enriched the cities which John knew in Asia Minor, but even so, his vision is wonderfully up to date. He assumes that every culture and every human achievement will find fulfilment in the city of God: nothing valuable nor good will be lost.

4. *John's city is built on reconciliation*. Such a universal city can only grow out of reconciliation between the nations. John knew a

good deal about human conflict: he was in prison when he saw his vision, a victim of the jealous tyranny of the Roman Empire. But he hoped in God. So he saw 'the river of the water of life, sparkling like crystal, flowing down the middle of the city's street'. The leaves of the trees which stood on its banks served (like medicine) for the healing of the nations.

5. *John's city is the gift of God.* In John's vision the city is not built by the labours of men. It is the gift of God, for the heavenly city 'comes down out of heaven from God'. There is, in this phrase, a deliberate contrast with the Old Testament parable-story of Babel, the city which men tried to build to their own design and by their own strength. 'Come,' they said, 'let us build ourselves a city and a name for ourselves.' Babel was destroyed, and God answered human arrogance by calling Abraham to leave the shelter of the Mesopotamian cities, with the great ziggurats which men built for their gods, and to live in the land of Palestine, as a nomad tent-dweller in dependence upon him alone.[11]

Perhaps this is one of the fundamental lessons that human beings have to learn today about their future. They are learning it painfully, but slowly and surely. They are discovering that human life cannot be truly lived without dependence upon God. It is in wonder and in worship, in trust and obedience to ultimate truth, that men discover the courage and persistence, the insights and the inspiration which they need to make their dreams come true. This is why the religions of mankind have played such a creative role in the Ascent of Man.

John's dream city is illuminated by the glory of God made known in Christ. 'The city had no need of sun or moon to shine upon it; for the glory of God gave it light, and its light was the Lamb.' At the heart of its life was the worship of God and of Christ. 'The throne of God and of the Lamb will be there, and his servants shall worship him; they shall see him face to face, and bear his name on their foreheads' (22.3-4).

We cannot have the city of our dreams without its worship. Men have tried to do so. They have placed all kinds of buildings at the centre of their cities – parliament buildings, royal and presidential palaces – universities – banks and stock exchanges – and they have come short of all they hoped for and all they dreamed of. John's dream is of a city illuminated by the presence of God and planned to centre on worship. The recovery of this emphasis is a priority for contemporary men and women. Not because politics and economics, art and culture mean nothing, but because they only play their true part when they are inspired and guided by transcendent goals and values.

Here or there, now or then?

In the previous two sections, I have deliberately set two visions of the future side by side, and in immediate succession:

The hope for world-community (expressed in terms of our present human existence, by such diverse thinkers as Martin Luther King and the Club of Rome)	*The vision of the new Jerusalem* (declared by John, and other Bible writers,[12] to be the creation and gift of God)

Superficially these two visions have much in common: they are visions of the future, they involve the whole human race, their aims are peace, justice and the reconciliation of particular interests in the goal of universal well-being.

The similarities are such that many people would say that the two visions are two ways of expressing the same hope, one in secular terms and the other in terms which look to God for the fulfilment of their dreams. Nevertheless, religious people have always felt difficulty in identifying the two visions in this simple way. The devout Muslim, for example, is taught on the one hand to attribute every event to the will of God, so that for him the world already is the place where God's will is being effected: on the other hand, Islam also lays much emphasis upon the judgment day when God will intervene to judge the living and the dead and to determine the destiny, not of nations, but of individuals. The Buddhist's goal is, through a series of earthly existences, to gain *nirvana* where one's own individual consciousness is absorbed into the great being of the Absolute. The devout Muslim or Buddhist, therefore, finds it difficult to relate the vision of a world-community realized on earth to the ultimate purposes of God. For them *heaven* and *earth* are separate realities.

Christians, however, believe that God's Word became one with mankind in the person of Jesus Christ: this makes it easier for them to affirm the relationship which these two visions have with each other, and which is expressed in the similarities between them. There is not, however, a common mind among Christians about this, and a discussion of these different attitudes may help to clarify the relationship between these two visions of the future.

Some Christians would lay so much emphasis upon God's initiative in bringing the new Jerusalem into being that they discount any human contribution to the building of that city. Moreover, they would say that it is an affair of the supernatural, spiritual order: the new Jerusalem lies entirely beyond our present world of space and time. Christians are called to be 'citizens of heaven', and 'Christ's kingdom does not belong to this world'.[13] In contrast with the heavenly city, all efforts to build human cities are doomed in the long run to failure because of human sinfulness.

This attitude takes many forms. It is most clearly expressed perhaps in John Bunyan's great book, *Pilgrim's Progress*, which describes how the message of the gospel is given to the individual Christian, while he passes through this world on his way towards the heavenly city. The real destiny of men and women lies beyond life upon this earth, and Christians are called to pass through it as strangers and as pilgrims. According to this view, the fundamental problems of life are those which arise from a person's individual responsibility towards God and the church's task is to bring a person into touch with Christ so that he or she may receive forgiveness and the new life of the Holy Spirit. When a person has been converted in that way, his task is to win others to the same experience and to grow himself in the virtues of Christian discipleship. In this way, people are prepared for life with God in the eternal world which lies beyond our physical existence and is discontinuous with it.

Many Christians who take this view believe that Christians also have a responsibility towards the society in which they live, and act accordingly. This was made clear, for example, in the Covenant which was endorsed at the close of the International Congress on World Evangelism held at Lausanne in July 1974.

> The salvation we claim should be transforming us in the totality of our personal and social responsibilities . . . We need to break out of our ecclesiastical ghettoes and permeate non-Christian society . . . Those of us who live in affluent circumstances accept our duty to develop a simple life-style in order to contribute more generously to both relief and evangelism.

Those who wrote the Covenant, however, also made it clear that for them world evangelization is still the primary task for Christians, and that evangelism means introducing people to a personal experience of Christ which will reach fulfilment in the future kingdom of God.

In the church's mission of sacrificial service evangelism is primary . . . Evangelism itself is the proclamation of the historical, biblical Christ as Saviour and Lord, with a view to persuading people to come to him personally and so be reconciled to God . . . We believe that Jesus Christ will return personally and visibly, in power and glory, to consummate his salvation and his judgment . . . We therefore reject as a proud self-confident dream the notion that man can ever build a utopia on earth. Our Christian confidence is that God will perfect his kingdom and we look forward with eager anticipation to that day, and to the new heaven and earth in which righteousness will dwell and God will reign for ever.[14]

Although those who wrote the Covenant made great efforts to do justice to the social responsibilities of Christians, and of the church, they had no hesitation in emphasizing the supernatural nature of God's coming kingdom. If they were pressed to do so, they would probably describe the two visions, which we have been considering, as belonging to two separate spheres of existence, the earthly and the heavenly. In contrast with their attitude, other Christians would describe the two visions as complementary ways of looking at one world. This view is supported by many who labour in the harsh conditions of poor urban communities, or in areas where famine, malnutrition and cruel poverty make life itself a burden and a humiliation. The first priorities for them in working for the kingdom of God are the provision of food, of shelter, and of freedom. In providing them, people discover the reality of the new Jerusalem, and begin to build it here and now upon earth.

The writings of Pierre Teilhard de Chardin, the great Jesuit scholar who was also priest and poet, have helped many Christians to integrate their understanding of God's purpose in creation with their scientific understanding of natural evolution. His writings are often difficult to interpret, because of their breadth of vision, but here is a passage which appears to merge these two visions within the great perspective of God's evolutionary design.

We always tend to forget that the supernatural is a leaven, a life-principle, not a complete organism. Its purpose is to transform 'nature'; and it cannot do that apart from the material with which nature presents it. If the Hebrews kept their gaze fixed for three thousand years on the coming of the Messiah it was because they saw him effulgent with the glory of their own people. If St Paul's disciples lived in a constant eager yearning for the great day of the second coming of Christ it was because they looked to the Son of Man to give them a personal, tangible solution to the problems and the injustices of earthly life. The expectation of heaven cannot be kept alive unless it is made flesh. With what body, then, shall our own be clothed?

With an immense, *completely human* hope.[15]

As is so often the case, it seems that we should look for the truth in this matter not in one or other of the two attitudes which we have discussed in the preceding paragraphs but in one which holds their different visions of the truth together in creative tension.

On the one hand, Christians cannot ignore contemporary social problems or the solutions which are proposed to solve them. As Dr Michael Ramsey said when he was Archbishop of Canterbury:

> It is right for Christian people to strive for justice for the poor and hungry people in the world, for the abolition of discrimination between races in any society and for the human rights of freedom of opinion and of belief and religion. The kingdom of God upon earth includes the rule of God's righteousness in every part of human life, and Christians affirm this whenever they pray 'Thy Kingdom come'.[16]

Christians work for the doing of God's will in their everyday lives and that means within the environment in which they live. Some will be concerned with immediate social problems: others will have opportunity to concern themselves with broader issues on a national or world scale.

On the other hand, Christians do not believe that God's will and purpose will come to final fulfilment within the created universe of space and time. Together with people of other faiths, they worship God as the Eternal Being whose life and being transcend the created universe. They dare to believe that, in receiving the grace of God's Spirit, they are given the privilege of participating in the eternal life of God. Our human condition is always marked by uncertainty, insecurity and imperfection, and it is the Christian's hope that at the boundary between time and eternity God will make all things new, and give his creatures that vision of himself which is pure joy. Even in our moments of greatest happiness, and even when we are most closely involved with earthly affairs, we look beyond ourselves to the Eternal God who retains fulfilment as a gift still to be given. This great hope will always be an essential element in the church's message.

The Christian, therefore, is asked to see these two great visions, that of the secular world-community, and that of the new Jerusalem, as complementary expressions of the one divine will. On the one hand, he is called to affirm the growth towards a world community of justice and peace as that which is willed by God, and to which he must give of his best during his time on earth: and yet, even in this act of affirmation, he is to keep his eyes on the ultimate fulfilment which is the divine gift and not the fruit of human endeavour. He is called to hope for that unseen world to which God will call his own, which lies beyond space and time; and yet, even in this act of hoping, to recognize that in that transcendent world there will be fulfilment of all the visions and endeavours of the developing world in which we now live. The secular hope for world-community and the vision of the new Jerusalem complement each other and merge together, but their boundaries do not coincide.

This double attitude is well illustrated by the following quotations taken from the Taizé quarterly *Communion*. They are particularly valuable because they are taken from occasional writings, and were not written to answer theological questions.

If we set out in quest of God, Christ summons us to involve our entire being in the effort to create the harmony of the Kingdom. There will be stark seeking in the desert silence; journeys leading through the struggles and contradictions of human realities; the discovery of new paths in art or science. Christ proclaims his Kingdom to be like a precious pearl, worth giving everything up for, choosing the best . . . Many are the ways it urges us along. But all of them seem to be expressions of a *double reality*: trustful surrender to the Invisible, Eternal, Universal; and life deliberately chosen in terms of our people's deepest hopes (Paolo Bagattini, Italy).

Our love will carry us, like clippers of the past, towards the unknown shores of a future sharing, towards the Church of God, the anticipation of that glorious city we look towards in the light of eternity . . . Out on the world's high seas, in the midst of God's People, at the heart of our struggles, we shall seek the pearl of great price: the face of Him who loved us first, and who even died for that love (Moiz Rasiwala, India).[17]

3 Salt to the World

The kingdom of God

In the last section of the previous chapter we discussed the ambivalent attitude which Christians have towards the contemporary world. On the one hand they affirm it as the sphere in which God's kingdom is to be proclaimed and his will is to be done; on the other hand, they value it as the prelude to a yet more glorious manifestation of his kingdom which transcends the natural world and is yet to come. This double attitude is present throughout the Bible, but more clearly in the New Testament than in the Old.

The Old Testament, in fact, tells how God dealt with one particular nation during the ups and downs of its history. The prophets did not preach about salvation as if it were something which would be found in another world, but as a condition of well-being, prosperity and fulfilment which people would find, during their earthly lives, in a Jerusalem ruled by the Law of God. It was only towards the end of the Old Testament period that this hope developed into belief that the dead also would share through resurrection in the hoped for time of salvation.[1] The inclusion of the Old Testament, therefore, within the Christian Bible should be enough to convince Christians that the living God is concerned with justice and righteousness in everyday life. 'Let justice roll on like a river and righteousness like an ever-flowing stream' (Amos 5.24) is a central theme in the preaching of all the prophets.

It is in the New Testament, and especially in the teaching of Jesus about the kingdom of God, that we find confirmation of the double attitude towards human destiny which I have suggested is the proper one for Christians to adopt. God's kingly authority, Jesus taught, is a living reality in the contemporary world and the most important factor in the human environment: as such, it should determine how people ought to live now. The 'kingly rule of God' was in fact the

23

basic theme of his teaching, and St Mark summarized Jesus' ministry in these words: 'Jesus came into Galilee proclaiming the Gospel of God: "The time has come; the kingdom of God is upon you; repent, and believe the Gospel."' The 'good news about the kingdom of God' meant 'good news for the poor, release for prisoners, recovery of sight for the blind, freedom for the down trodden'. Jesus came as 'the king of peace in the name of the Lord' and the tragedy was that his contemporaries did not 'recognize God's moment when it came': it had been 'within their grasp' and they let it slip. His acts of healing also were signs of the presence of God's kingdom: 'If it is by the finger of God that I drive out the devils, then be sure the kingdom of God has already come upon you,' said Jesus.[2]

Because God's rule is so important, Jesus called upon people to repent and to turn away from evil. God's rule is not something in the distant future, for God is already present as king. People must be prepared at any time to give account of their lives to God: they must be ready to give up everything else in order to win a share in his kingdom (Matt. 15.24–8). Only those who keep God's laws in their inmost thoughts truly love him: those who do this, and search for God's kingdom in all things, are the people who are truly happy. To find out God's will and to do it is the most important thing in life. Jesus made God's rule the one aim of his whole life and he spent long hours in quiet prayer. 'My food', he said, 'is to do the will of him who sent me and to accomplish his work' (John 4.34).

At the end, our Lord handed on his responsibility for God's kingdom to his disciples: 'they had stood firmly by him in his times of trial and he vested in them the kingship which his Father had vested in him.' The power of this kingship was manifested after the resurrection when 'Christ was exalted at God's right hand: he received the Holy Spirit from the Father, as was promised, and all that men saw and heard in the ministry of the Church flowed from him.' As his apostles, or commissioned representatives, they also went about telling the good news of the contemporary reign of God.[3]

Although he was committed to seeking God's kingdom in the contemporary world, Jesus also looked forward to a future fulfilment of God's will to take place on his initiative. He expressed this hope by speaking about the coming in glory of the Son of Man, God's appointed vice-regent, and the hour of judgment. 'Like the lightning-flash that lights up the earth from end to end, the Son of Man will be when his day comes.' 'They will see the Son of Man coming on a cloud with great power and glory . . . Be on the alert, praying at all times for strength to pass safely through these imminent troubles and to stand in the presence of the Son of Man.' To stand in his presence on Judgment Day would involve an impartial scrutiny of all life's actions and attitudes. The three Synoptic Gospels show that Jesus warned his hearers at all periods of his ministry about Judgment Day and the coming of the Son of Man associated with it.[4]

To put this in summary form, Jesus taught that the kingly rule of God is a living reality, and that its glory and power are demonstrated in three separate but related ways:

1. in the ministry of Jesus, in which he healed the sick and taught the way of God's kingdom;
2. in the ministry of his disciples, who share with him in the authority of God's kingdom;
3. in the great events of the Day of Judgment: these will occur on the divine initiative and demonstrate God's sovereignty in a final and all-inclusive way.

The Christian, therefore, can neither identify this world with the kingdom of God, nor separate the one from the other. The world of history and the world of fulfilment are held together within the will and the purpose of God.

> The kingdom is *this* world seen in the light of that relationship with God which underlines and penetrates all life and all relationships. It is, as it were, the name of the game of living, striving, loving, a name which signifies that these realities have both an immanent divine source and a transcendent future towards which they must be kept open.[5]

The fundamental unity which underlies these different aspects of the kingdom of God is affirmed in the incarnation and the resurrection. The incarnation, made visible to human eyes on the first Christmas Day, binds together the transcendent kingdom of God with the contingent world of creation in the one loving and caring life of Jesus. The Eternal Word became flesh, not in order to rescue men out of the human existence which his sharing in it made holy, but in order to make that same flesh beautiful with the glory of God. The resurrection of the first Easter Day brought the reality of God's eternal kingdom within the experience of the disciples and gave them a foretaste of the glory yet to come. 'A real experience of the dawning of God's new world stood at the beginning of the history of the church.'

Thus the disciples of Christ are called to become involved in 'the great stream of life', to commit themselves wholeheartedly with others to the human adventure, to stand with their contemporaries at the turning point of history, and to work for the coming of a new age. But their contribution will have two qualities of great value. They will work wholeheartedly for justice, peace and progress in the confidence that the powers of God's kingdom are at work in the natural world to achieve his purposes. They will also have their eyes on the ultimate horizon of God's final glory, and see intermediate horizons in the light of it.

The road

In the gospels, Jesus associated the kingdom with repentance, that is with a change of attitude towards the priorities of life,[7] and this call for repentance is echoed in contemporary assessments of the human situation. The Club of Rome's report, *The Limits to Growth*, for example, to which we have already referred, concluded: 'We affirm finally that any deliberate attempt to reach a rational and enduring state of equilibrium ... must ultimately be founded on a basic change of values and goals at individual, national and world levels.'[8] Again, when the Nobel Foundation called a special conference in 1970 to discuss 'The Place of Values in a World òf Facts', Professor Arne Tiselius, who opened it, spoke of 'a growing awareness among people of all nations that something is wrong with the world and that there is an urgent need to come together to see what should be done.'

Gordon Rattray Taylor has documented the call, which is made by many commentators, to reassess the human situation in a chapter of his book, *Rethink*, which he calls 'The Receding Utopia'. His most moving quotation is from a fifteen year old Texan boy, Shannon Dixon: 'We see the world as a huge rumble as it goes by with wars, poverty, prejudice, and the lack of understanding among people and nations. Then we stop and think: there must be a better way and we have to find it ... The answer is out there somewhere. We need to reach for it ...' Taylor himself sums up his long analysis of the readjustment going on in the thinking of Western society, with these words: 'How can we make quality of life, rather than power or profit or gimmickry, the criterion of all our choices? That is the paramount question for the next half century.'[9]

Christians are called to share in this questioning with others. Indeed their belief that the kingdom of God is something yet to come gives them a particular responsibility to ask questions about the direction in which human society is moving and evolving. But they ask questions hopefully, for they recognize the presence within history of God's Spirit, guiding evolution towards the fulfilment of the divine purpose. In a special way, his influence has been associated with the many expressions of God's Word, and these provide answers to the most serious of human questions. These answers make up the gospel with which Christians are entrusted.

Before we go on to discuss these answers in the following chapters, however, let us understand clearly how they are disclosed to Christians and those with whom they share them. The Bible bears witness to them, but they are not just written in a book for the casual reader to stumble upon them. The church bears witness to them, but they are not a possession of the church for the church to dispense in sacrament and counsel on conditions of the church's choosing. Christians, whether as individuals or as groups, discover the gospel answers only as they themselves face the questions which are asked in the contemporary world and struggle with them.

In a book published during the dark days of the 1939–45 war, John Mackay, President of Princeton University, USA, contrasted two types of theologians; those of the balcony and those of the road.[10] Those of the balcony are those who work out their theology at a distance from ordinary everyday life, observing its movement and its actors like people in Spain who sit on their upstairs balconies in the evenings and watch life go by on the street below. The theology which they produce is often of fine quality, by standards of academic scholarship, but it is remote from ordinary life, authoritarian and cold. In contrast with them, the theologians of the road are those who share fully in the hustle and bustle of the streets, who give themselves to the dust, the sweat and the tediousness of travel, and who work out their answers as they walk along in company with others, sharing their burdens. They resemble the 'barefoot doctors' of modern China. Jesus, the carpenter of Nazareth, was a theologian like that: he worked out his theology in the company of his friends and neighbours, and he called his disciples to come and follow him along the road of life. The first name given to the church by people outside its membership was 'the people of the road': it is there, on the road of everyday life, that questions are asked which really matter, and relevant answers are discovered for them.[11]

The catholic presence of the church

People all across the world are being drawn together in the search for answers to questions about human destiny. Mankind itself has reached a turning point in its development and there are many problems which can only be properly discussed across national and ideological boundaries. International conferences about major areas of human concern, such as food, resources, development, peace, take place at frequent intervals. Many politicians and their advisers spend long hours travelling from one top-level discussion to another. It is important, therefore, to notice how 'catholic' the church is becoming in the original 'territorial' meaning of that word.

In a world where men are seeking to build a community which will transcend national and cultural frontiers, there are Christian churches in almost every country, and there are congregations living and witnessing in most important cities, (with, of course, some exceptions). This world-wide growth of the church is not the achievement of any particular communion or denomination and we might well say of it: 'It is the Lord's doing and it is marvellous in our eyes.' There are more Christians in the world than the adherents of any other single religion and this is a fact well worth pondering.

In some places, especially in countries like Arabia and Afghanistan which have been isolated for centuries, Christians are few in numbers and mostly expatriates. In other countries Christianity is the religion of a minority only and Islam, Buddhism, or Hinduism is dominant. In China, the country with the largest population in the world, Christians are very few in number. These facts should cause us to pause before making too optimistic statements about the significance of the Christian church on the world scene. Nevertheless in many areas, churches are large in numbers and of some importance, and this not only in Western Europe or the Americas. It is said, for example, that in Korea 10% of the population are Christians and in Indonesia church membership is growing at the rate of 25% each year. Even in Eastern Europe, the churches have, in many places, a strong and vigorous life as Trevor Beeson has shown in his book *Discretion and Valour*.[12] The most remarkable growth of the churches is in Africa and Dr David Barrett has demonstrated that, if the present rate of increase continues, Christians in Africa will number 350,000,000 people by AD 2,000. He wrote: 'We are witnessing in this century the rise of a fifth massive pulsation or surge in Christian history, the most startling component of which is the meteoric rise of the church in Black Africa.'[13]

As examples of this remarkable growth we might mention that the Anglican dioceses in the Province of West Africa have grown in number as follows: 1963, ten dioceses: 1974, seventeen dioceses: 1977, twenty-one. In Enugu, Eastern Nigeria, where some thirty years ago one Roman Catholic priest paid a monthly visit, there is now a seminary of that church with 450 students, and a faculty of twelve teachers all but one of whom are Nigerian. The first Anglican convert in the Sudan, John e Thor, was baptized in 1916: today there are four Sudanese bishops in that church assisted by over a hundred priests.

The growth of the churches and the 'catholic' dimension of their presence throughout the world are reasons for hope. At a time when nations are becoming much more dependent on each other for the supply of food and natural resources, and all human societies are confronted by the same basic problems, there are significant groups of people in almost every part of the world who share the same convictions about the meaning and purpose of human existence and the principles on which true community may be built. Moreover the leadership of this great complex of churches is a multi-racial one which reflects the aspirations and hopes of Third World churches as well as of the older established churches of Europe and America. Their united leadership could contribute a great deal to the development of world community.

Dr Barrett in the article which I quoted above spoke of 'the rise in this century of a fifth massive pulsation or surge in Christian history'. I believe that this is a valid hope, provided that the churches are true to their Lord, and open towards each other. This present advance may become as great and as far-reaching in its effects as that which took the apostles out of rural, provincial Palestine into the cosmopolitan, Greek-speaking cities of the Roman Empire. But it will not come unless the churches throughout the world can find true community between themselves. If they can, then the churches could again become a living force towards community within the family of nations.

This hope fills me with joy and expectation. I admit, of course, that there are many disappointing features in the life of the churches and particularly in the recent lack of progress towards their unity in life and in mission. Not only do the differences between catholic and protestant churches persist, but there are also serious differences between the so-called 'liberals' and 'conservatives', between 'radicals' and 'traditionalists', between the historic churches and those which are independent or charismatic. These divisions are serious, but they appear less threatening if the church is seen within the long perspectives of history. In the light of that time scale, one notices the growing emergence of the concept of 'world community', on a scale and to a degree never previously imagined, and matched to it in the providence of God, companies of men and women, of every race and nation, almost of every tribe and language, who name one Lord and are committed, despite their organizational divisions, to walk one way. Christians believe that God's eternal purposes were achieved by one man, a peasant carpenter, dying on a cross outside a city wall: what can he not do with the nine hundred million or so who serve him now if they are true to their Lord?

God – universe – church

In seeking answers to the questions which are asked on the road of our contemporary world, Christians are concerned with three great realities; God, the natural universe, and the church. They do not always see clearly the relationships between them.

God is the living being who is always there, the Other who is present with all persons and things, and yet who is also beyond them. He is the Eternal You who addresses us and all others at the heart of our experience.

The natural universe is that which exists in God's presence and by his will. It comprises the whole vast range of natural substances and energies and all living creatures. It spans the whole of space and stretches across the long distances of time. It is a universe of existence so vast that no scientific research has ever reached its frontiers, whether of space or time, or fully analysed its constituent elements. Within this vast universe, human beings are, of course, primarily concerned with planet earth and their own evolution and development upon it.

The church, the third of our realities, is itself part of the natural universe: its members belong to human society and like their fellows live in and by means of the same natural environment. Its members, however, find the *raison d'être* of their community in a unique event which they believe links together in a new relationship the two realities which I have already mentioned, namely God and the natural universe. They believe that in Jesus Christ God became incarnate in the natural world, in one unique human life. They believe that this event has significance for the whole life of mankind, and ultimately for the whole universe. They believe that in their own community, whose members acknowledge the lordship of Christ, the power of God is present in a particular way to bring his purposes to a fulfilment which transcends the development of the natural universe.

God, the natural universe and the church are thus inextricably linked together, and it will be helpful, as an introduction to the following chapters, to consider the relationship between them. Christians sometimes assume that God is primarily concerned with the church and its members, and only secondarily with the world in which the church lives. This, however, is contrary to the teaching of our Lord and his apostles, for they showed themselves to be concerned with the needs of the whole human community and not simply with those of the church and its members. In this present period of crisis and opportunity it is of the utmost importance that the churches should get their priorities right and direct their attention outwards towards the world.

Consider the selfless generosity of Jesus: his willingness to risk his reputation by sharing meals with the tax-gatherers and irreligious: his leaving Capernaum, where his preaching and healing had great success, in order to preach in the other villages of Galilee: his determination to go up to Jerusalem in the face of opposition and danger.[14] Jesus was 'the man for others', who spent his few years of ministry not only with a close group of disciples who treasured his teaching, but out on the hillsides of Galilee and in the houses of men like Matthew and Zacchaeus. When he visited the synagogue or the temple, he was often moved to confront the religious leaders of his day, or to heal those who were in need. He was preoccupied with concern for the people and he saw his role towards them to be that of shepherd, of fisherman, and farmer. 'The sight of the people moved him to pity: they were like sheep without a shepherd, harassed and helpless; and he said to his disciples, "The crop is heavy, but labourers are scarce; you must therefore beg the owner to send labourers to harvest his crop"' (Matt. 9.36–8). His longing was to team up with those who were burdened with the cares of life, and to sustain their weaknesses with his own strength (Matt. 11.28–30).

'Like master, like servant.' The disciples were called to be his apprentices: he, the master craftsman, would train them in the crafts of fishing for men, of shepherding those in need. The metaphors which Christ used to describe his disciples' ministry in the world were in keeping with the training which he gave them as they walked Galilee with him. He declared that they would be 'salt to the world' giving up their own vitality and virtue to make the world purer and of better flavour. They were to be 'light for all the world', and there

31

can be no light without the expenditure of energy (this was especially so in peasant Palestine where the oil lamps were fed by the oil taken at harvest time from the olives and carefully stored: every time a lamp was lit, household stores were depleted). He, their Lord, had come to serve others and he called his apprentices to do the same. No one whose feet had been washed by Jesus could have had any doubt about his calling to serve others generously and selflessly.[15]

We have already seen in the previous chapter how John found room in his great vision of the new Jerusalem for the fulfilment of all that is great in the histories of the nations: 'The wealth and splendour of the nations shall be brought into it'. This wide outlook was shared by the apostles, and it is a constant theme in their writings. They were the pastors of small communities of Christians living in the great cities of the eastern Mediterranean, and separated from each other by long distances and difficult travel, but they never lost the belief that God's purposes of love were for the universe. They were not preoccupied with the problems of the new churches though they gave them their attention; they were preoccupied rather with the task of making God's gifts of grace known to the human communities of which they were members. To share those gifts was to proclaim the gospel of God's kingdom and to have a share in the mission of God. It is a mission which reaches to the ends of the earth.[16]

4 Amazing Grace

The Ground of all Being

The whole universe exists in the presence of God, and lives by his will. What this means to God is, of course, beyond the capabilities of finite creatures either to conceive or to imagine. The Being of God is a mystery which no finite minds can ever hope to penetrate. Sensitivity towards this mystery has led mystics all through the ages to express their deepest thoughts about God in negative terms – not because God is negative, but rather because he is so alive, so glorious, so overwhelming in every respect that human speech comes nowhere near any appropriateness in speaking of him. The Qur'an expresses this truth in words directed towards the pagan Arabs who called some of their lesser deities 'daughters of God'.

> Say: He is (the only) God, the Unique:
> God, the Eternal:
> He neither begat, nor was begotten:
> Not one being is adequate to match him.

This short chapter is properly called 'the Chapter of Sincere Religion'.[1]

But although God is beyond human comprehension or analysis, human beings live by his will and are aware of his presence. In prayer and worship, in contemplation and meditation, by acts of piety and of faith, men and women reach out to the Ground of their Being and enter into meaningful relations with him.

The evidence for this lies all across the pages of human history until our own times. It is impossible now to reconstruct the earliest religious acts of human people, but as soon as human history becomes documented by archaeological or literary remains, it becomes clear that religion is an integral element in human lives. The many books published on comparative religion make this clear. The writers may differ in their explanations or analysis of the different religions, but they agree at least in recognizing the important place which religious faith and religious practice have always had in human society.

To draw attention to the almost universal practice of religion does not, of course, prove the truths of religion nor the existence of God. This is a question which cannot be argued in any detail in a book like this, but it may be helpful to make a few comments.

First, if we deny that religious truth has a sound basis, we must assume that all through history human beings have been the victims of illusion, and this is very difficult to contemplate. 'If the souls and spirits and gods of religion are regarded as complete illusions, then some biological, psychological or sociological theory of how everywhere and at all times men have been stupid enough to believe in them seems to be called for.' Professor Evans-Pritchard, who made that comment towards the end of his *Theories of Primitive Religion* [2], went on to point out that, in contrast with the non-believer, the believer is better equipped to understand religious practices because he recognizes the reality to which they refer. In this connection, he quoted the words of another distinguished anthropologist, William Schmidt: 'If religion is essentially of the inner life, it follows that it can be truly grasped only from within. But beyond a doubt, this can be better done by one in whose inward consciousness an experience of religion plays a part. There is but too much danger that the other (the non-believer) will talk of religion as a blind man might of colours, or one totally devoid of ear, of a beautiful musical composition.' [3]

Secondly, whatever may be said about religion in human society in general, it is mainly in modern industrial society (of the West but also increasingly in the East) that religion appears irrelevant or ineffective. Western Christians live in a secular world, that is to say, in a community which is preoccupied with the demands of the present moment in terms of life in this physical universe alone. Pressures like those which we discussed in chapter 1 allow people little leisure to become aware of realities and influences which go beyond their immediate environment. Other pressures also increase their insensitivity towards them: the assumption that science explains everything in measurable, finite terms, the emphasis of the consumer society upon material pleasures and possessions, and the preoccupation of economists, politicians, and sociologists with the pressing but ever-changing and transient problems of our time. Thus many people today have lost, or are in danger of losing their awareness of God's presence. Any talk about religion appears at first sight meaningless to them, and the message of hope which Christians long to proclaim is unintelligible to them: for them it rings no bells, it 'scratches where they have no itch'.

But thirdly, although the secular attitudes of industrial, urban society present a serious challenge to the survival of religion, it need not be assumed that this challenge will in the long run be successful. Some evidence indeed points the other way and suggests that there may soon be a recovery of religious faith and practice, even in the Western world. This is suggested by the growing interest in meditation and contemplation, and by the way in which young people are attracted, 'turned on' as they say, by the person of Jesus. Moreover, science itself no longer claims to provide complete and final answers to the questions which we ask about the universe. 'What physics has done is to show that (the method of the artist) is the only method to knowledge. There is no absolute knowledge. And those who claim it, whether they are scientists or dogmatists, open the door to tragedy. All information is imperfect. We have to treat it with humility. That is the human condition; and that is what quantum physics says.'[4]

The religious attitude to life is not in fact alien to the human adventure even at the heights of scientific and technological achievement. When the American astronauts in the rocket Apollo XIII, which was nearly wrecked on its way to the moon in September 1970, landed safely in the Pacific, they were picked up by the US aircraft-carrier Iwojima. On its deck, in view of the world's television cameras, they bowed their heads while the ship's chaplain said a short prayer of thanksgiving. Many people joined them in their prayer, and found nothing incongruous in doing so. Indeed, it might be said that that very action, simple though it was, made their adventure something which could be shared by others in the human community.

Many people evaluate religion as nothing more than a psychic projection by human beings of their own needs to relate better to the supernatural forces which they see at work in the world, or of their desires for security and fulfilment. This approach concentrates attention on the inner thought-processes of the human person, and does not do justice to the complex realities of the religious relationship. It is a better interpretation of the facts to describe religion as *response* by human people to the mysteries with which their lives are surrounded and which they associate with the living God.

The different religious adventures of mankind bear witness to the variety and range of that response. Their united witness is to the existence of a Being who is in a constant living relationship with the universe of which he is the Creator and the Ground of its Being. Whatever the differences between them, the living reign of God throughout the whole universe is a constant theme which runs through them all as the following extracts show.

> He it is who forges the thunder and creates the wind,
> who showers abundant rain on the earth,
> who darkens the dawn with thick clouds,
> and marches over the heights of the earth –
> his name is the Lord the God of Hosts.
>
> (Amos, Hebrew prophet, about 750 BC) [5]

Why should they not revere You? . . . You are first Creator, Infinite, Lord of the gods, home of the universe. You are the Imperishable. You are what is and what is not and what is greater than both . . . You are the last prop-and-resting-place of this universe. You are the knower and what is to be known . . . The whole universe was spun by You . . . Your strength is infinite, your power is limitless. You bring all things to their fulfilment: hence You are All . . . You are the father of the world of moving and unmoving things.

(Ancient Hindu Scripture of about 500–100 BC) [6]

His is the power and the kingdom and the glory and the majesty and to Him belongs creation and the rule over what He has created: He alone is the Giver of life, He is omniscient for His knowledge encompasses all things, from the deepest depths of the earth to the highest heights of the heavens. The smallest atom in the earth or the heavens is known unto Him. He is aware of how the ants creep upon the hard rock in the darkness of the night. He perceives the movement of specks of dust in the air. He beholds the thoughts which pass through the minds of men, and the range of their fancies and the secrets of their hearts, by His knowledge, which was from aforetime.

(From al-Ghazzali, a Muslim theologian who died in AD 1111) [7]

> God, supreme being, master of the earth,
> You that made all things,
> I am here and the reason I have come is to get strength
> in my life.
> That no wild animal may meet me,
> that the lightning may not find me out.
> That the sorcerer may not see me,
> that the man of evil intent may not look at me.
> God, Lord Tshitebwa Mukana.

> You, Kasongo on the sun side,
> Advance on your way, the earth is yours.
> (Contemporary prayer from the Baluba of Kasai, Africa) [8]

King and father

The testimony of all the religions is that *God lives* and *God reigns* and these truths were affirmed by Jesus. The basic theme of his teaching was 'the kingly rule of God' and we have already discussed what this meant for him, on pages 23ff. above. Jesus, however, added another dimension to the discussion about God's kingly rule, by teaching that his rule is one of loving compassion and boundless generosity.

According to Jesus, the care and compassion of God are for all the world. Thus, in response to complaints that he was sharing his teaching about God's kingdom with those groups in the community who were not particularly religious, and showing them friendship, he told three simple but revolutionary parables.

> God, he said, is like a shepherd who searches for a sheep which has strayed. The shepherd suffers hardship in doing this, and risks his life on the wild hills.

> God is like a careful housewife. She will turn the whole house upside down in order to find a coin which she has lost.

> God is like a father, who waits patiently for his foolish son to return home, and welcomes him unconditionally when he comes. [9]

According to Jesus, God has no favourites, but gives his love to all alike. These convictions led him to give his own life in teaching, preaching, and healing throughout Galilee and beyond. He brought the love and power of God to all who were in need, whether they were Jews or not. He invited them to enter into the reality of God's sovereign rule, and he declared that 'from east and west people will come, from north and south, for the feast in the kingdom of God' (Luke 13.29).

Jesus taught his disciples that if they wished to be true children of God they must reflect in their own behaviour the universal nature of God's love for the world. 'What I tell you is this: Love your enemies and pray for your persecutors; only so can you be children of your heavenly Father, who makes his sun rise on good and bad alike, and sends the rain on the honest and the dishonest. If you love only those who love you, what reward can you expect? Surely the tax-gatherers do as much as that. And if you greet only your brothers, what is there extraordinary about that? Even the heathen do as much. There must be no limit to your goodness, as your heavenly Father's goodness knows no bounds' (Matt. 5.44–8). 'You must love your enemies and do good; and lend without expecting any return; and you will have a rich reward: you will be sons of the Most High, because he himself is kind to the ungrateful and wicked. Be compassionate as your Father is compassionate' (Luke 6.35–6).

Jesus, as God's servant, was 'The Man for Others' who used his resources of prayer and care, of wisdom and compassion, to minister to those in need of any kind, and he asked his disciples for a similar generosity towards others. They also were called to a life of openness, greeting and serving those whom they met on the road of life, giving generously without stint, inviting the poor and deprived to their parties. Because Jesus practised such a generosity to all in need, regardless of their apparent status in the community or even whether they were Jews or not, his enemies brought him at last to the hill of Calvary. We shall discuss this in the next chapter. Meanwhile let me conclude this section by emphasizing that the generosity which Jesus practised and which he asked from his disciples was the consequence of his teaching about God. For Jesus, 'the kingdom of God' meant God present in and for his creation in gracious and compassionate love. The Ground of all Being, the Eternal God, is not only king, but father as well.

> If we ask what is this Kingdom of God that so dominates the life and words of Jesus and rides roughshod over established belief and practice, challenging all constituted authorities, the only answer is that it is the realisation of God's will in the world. It is God's will being done on earth as it is done in heaven. But what then is this will of God? For Pharisaic Judaism it was holiness and righteousness as revealed in the Law . . . For many (Jews) the Kingdom of God meant the downfall of Rome and the exaltation of Israel to world-dominion. For Jesus the will of God is primarily the forgiving, reconciling, redeeming love of God.[10]

These words of T. W. Manson are echoed by those of a contemporary New Testament scholar, Joachim Jeremias: 'The decisive element may be summarized briefly: the chief characteristic of the new people of God gathered together by Jesus is their awareness of the boundlessness of God's grace.'[11]

Christians believe that Jesus was the Word of God made man, and that he disclosed in a unique way the inner nature of God's kingdom. Origen, a Christian scholar of c. AD 200, put this very simply by saying in a way which the Greek language makes it easy to do: 'Jesus is the very Kingdom itself.' We see, in his ministry and his compassionate care for others, the characteristics of the divine compassion spelt out in terms of a human life. This was especially true of our Lord's actions during the last hours of his life when he did all he could to strengthen the courage of his disciples and to ensure that his suffering would not break them. Here is God's love in action, displayed in the words and actions of the heroic teacher who in the end died upon the cross. His living concern for others knew no boundaries and was qualified by no conditions.

The generous love of God which they saw demonstrated so clearly in the ministry of Jesus became the dominant theme in the preaching of the apostles. 'Everyone who loves is a child of God and knows God, but the unloving know nothing of God,' wrote St John. 'For God is love; and his love was disclosed to us in this, that he sent his only Son into the world to bring us life' (1 John 4.7–9). St Paul's favourite word for it was 'grace': Archbishop Donald Coggan defines this as 'the outgoing, forgiving activity of God, totally undeserved, to men and women who have gone wrong', and he calls it 'the theme regnant of the Epistles of St Paul.[12] St Paul had been brought up by the strict training of the rabbis to venerate the sacred Law and to strive to keep it, in all its details, with scrupulous care. He had thought of God as one whose favour was dependent upon a rigorous and exacting obedience to the Law. Through his conversion to the Christian faith his attitudes were completely changed. He became the apostle of grace, responding with a whole and ardent love to 'the Son of God who had loved him and given himself for him'. For him the grace of God was fully expressed in 'the generosity of our Lord Jesus Christ; he was rich, yet for our sake he became poor, so that through his poverty we might become rich'.[14]

From his conversion onwards, St Paul spent his life trying to awaken others to respond to the graciousness of God, and he saw the task of mission in terms of reconciliation. Reconciliation was an act of the divine initiative, expressed in the life and passion of Jesus, and it was the church's privilege to be associated with this reconciling and

39

healing love. 'God has reconciled us men to himself through Christ, and he has enlisted us in this service of reconciliation. What I mean is, that God was in Christ reconciling the world to himself, no longer holding men's misdeeds against them, and that he has entrusted us with the message of reconciliation. We come therefore as Christ's ambassadors. It is as if God were appealing to you through us: in Christ's name, we implore you, be reconciled to God!' (2 Cor. 5.18–20).

We normally associate the grace of God with the forgiveness and renewal which are Christ's gifts, as St Paul did. God's grace, however, is wider in scope than that, and, in one sense, all human beings are dependent upon it, whether they realize it or not. To live a human life, in joy and in gladness, does not depend primarily upon one's wealth or possessions, or upon one's status or nationality, but upon the grace of God which has made human life possible and enriches human society with all kinds of spiritual and other gifts. This is not to deny the grave hurt which sickness, or poverty, or oppression, can cause in human lives; they, however, belong to a different range of questions. In point of fact, human existence itself, with all the opportunities, privileges, and hope associated with it, are gratuitous gifts to us, and dependent upon developments which took place in the long millennia of prehistory. They are the fruit of God's gracious purposes within the evolutionary process, made possible by the billions of fellow-creatures who in the past have contributed to the universe in which we now live. The human community stands on the shoulders of the many other species who have flourished and sometimes perished in the evolution of planet Earth.

A dramatic illustration of this dependence was given by Sir Bernard Lovell in his 1975 Presidential Address to the British Association. Postulating that our present universe took its origin some 10,000 million years ago in a sudden expansion from a dense concentrate of primaeval material, Sir Bernard went on to say:

Indeed I am inclined to accept contemporary scientific evidence as indicative of a far greater degree of man's total involvement with the universe. The life which we know depends on a sensitive molecular balance; the properties of the atoms of the familiar elements are determined by a delicate balance of electrical and nuclear forces. These and the large scale uniformity and isotropy of the universe were probably determined by events which occurred in the first second of time . . . In the earliest moments of the expansion of the universe, a millionth of a second after the beginning, calculations indicate that the temperature was of the order of 10 million degrees and the fundamental particles of nature – protons, neutrons, electrons, and hyperons – existed with radiation as the controlling force. One second after the beginning, when the temperature had fallen to a few thousand million degrees there was a period when the ratio of protons to neutrons remained constant for a minute or so. This was the critical period when the natural constants determined the ultimate abundance of helium to hydrogen in the universe. It is an astonishing reflection that if the proton-neutron interaction were only a few per cent stronger then all the hydrogen in the primaeval condensate would have turned into helium in the early stages of expansion. No galaxies, no stars, no life would have emerged. It would be a universe forever unknowable by living creatures. The existence of a remarkable and intimate relationship between man, the fundamental constants of nature and the initial moments of space and time, seems to be an inescapable condition of our presence here together.[14]

There have, of course, been many other critical developments in the evolutionary process when the eventual emergence of the human species hung precariously in the balance.[15]

Scientific discussions of this kind do not prove the existence of God, but they underline the fact that all human beings are dependent for their very existence upon a gracious purpose within the processes of the natural universe. Dependence upon the natural processes for food, water, warmth, and health is as true for the wealthy city-dweller who possesses a house full of electronic gadgetry as it is for the African or Asian peasant farmer. People of all religions identify the Ground of all Being, the life-force of the universe, with the divine Spirit who enters into personal relations with human people. Christians do the same, but they affirm also that this living God is the God of grace who loves his creation generously and without condition.

Human dependence upon the grace of God is well expressed in the Lord's prayer, which is common to all Christians and begins with the words 'Our Father in Heaven', or simply 'Father'[16] This reflects the practice of Jesus himself who used the Aramaic word *Abba*, (or 'dear Father'), when praying. 'Abba' was a word which small children used in the home when addressing their father, and the apostles treasured their memory of how Jesus had used this word during his agony in the garden and while dying on the cross.[17] Jesus used it because it expressed the intimate relationship with God which he had gained, as far as his human experience was concerned, through long nights of prayer and constant attention to him.

There is a sense in which Christ's use of the term 'dear Father' can never be copied by any of his disciples, for it grew out of his unique relationship with God. Nevertheless, because he shared it with them, they are privileged to use it. 'Once, in a certain place, Jesus was at prayer. When he ceased, one of his disciples said, "Lord teach us to pray, as John taught his disciples." He answered, "When you pray, say,

> Father, hallowed be your Name,
> Your kingdom come,
> Your will be done,
> on earth as in heaven.
> Give us today our daily bread.
> Forgive us our sins
> as we forgive those who sin against us.
> Do not bring us to the time of trial
> but deliver us from evil." ' [18]

The Lord's prayer expresses, in summary form, the essentials of human existence in relation to the living God. It is a relationship which depends upon his graciousness, and is related to his purposes: it expresses a person's deepest needs, for sustenance, for acceptance, and for protection.

The Lord's prayer is not to be used lightly, for it is given to those who are Christ's disciples, and it can only be fully understood against the background of his teaching. Even so, the privilege of praying this prayer is the heritage of Christians of every church, and every locality: it expresses more than anything else their common status as his children. Its use transcends frontiers of race or class, and it is the common possession of a greater number of people than those who have been baptized. Potentially it belongs to the whole human race which God has created. To share this prayer with others involves helping each other to know the graciousness of the God to whom it is addressed, and to do that is to be involved in his mission.

Unarmed soldiers of peace

One of the most courageous and fruitful acts recorded in the Acts of the Apostles was that of Ananias when he came to St Paul, lying blind in his Damascus lodging. It was courageous because St Paul had gone to Damascus with the authority of the High Priest to arrest any Christians whom he found and bring them to Jerusalem. It bore fruit because it convinced St Paul that the generosity of Christ was active in the lives of his disciples, and so made his conversion doubly sure. The first three words of Ananias' speech were the important ones, and they bound the two men together in a bond of mutual trust and responsibility. 'Ananias entered the house, laid his hands on Saul (in blessing), and said, "*Saul, my brother*, the Lord Jesus has sent me to you" ' (Acts 9.17).

Christians have no monopoly of generosity towards others and the idea of brotherhood is a universal one which many people use, some sincerely, others for the sake of show or rhetoric. An instance of the former came movingly into the TV documentary, 'The Man Who Skied Down Everest'. At a critical point in the story after an accident in which six Sherpas had been killed on the great ice-barrier at the foot of the last ascent up the mountain, one of their relatives turned to the Japanese climbing team and said: 'We Sherpas will go on climbing for as long as our Japanese brothers need us.' Brotherhood is not the monopoly of Christians, yet because of the teaching of Jesus and their constant use of the prayer 'Our Father', they are called to practise brotherhood with seriousness and commitment. On many occasions they have done so. Let me share a few examples with you from my own experience of a church in Africa.

In early 1964, the government of the Sudan expelled all foreign missionaries from the three southern provinces of that country. There had been tension for some years between the peoples of the south, many of whom were Christians, and the Arabic-speaking peoples of the north who were mostly Muslims and, shortly after the expulsion, this tension erupted into bitter guerilla warfare. When the Anglican Church Secretary bade farewell at the airport to his ex-patriate bishop to whom the expulsion order was then applied, he must have felt isolated, vulnerable, and tempted to be very bitter. But as he shook the bishop's hand, he murmured 'Father, forgive them, they know not what they do'. It is not surprising that the final peace agreement between north and south, which was signed in Addis Ababa nearly ten years later, owed much to the initiative and perseverance of the All Africa Council of Churches. Colonel Numeiry, the Sudanese President, paid a moving tribute to the Christians at that time when he called them 'the unarmed soldiers of peace'. The Peace Agreement was counter-signed by Canon Burgess Carr, Secretary of the All Africa Council of Churches, who had spent the whole night in prayer before the signing.

Such an initiative on behalf of the Council of Churches was only possible because those whom the Council represented were willing to seek for brotherhood. One of the factors which began to make for

43

peace was the generosity with which Christian women, living as so many southern Sudanese then did in an isolated area of the forest, suckled the babies of an Arab woman, when a civil aeroplane crashed in the bush. They and other survivors were eventually handed over safe and sound to the Arab authorities. Their attitude was in keeping with those of many others such as a young teacher called Ezibon Dalaka. Ezibon took his vocation to teach with the utmost serious-ness and he spared no effort to win for himself a clearer vision of truth, by reading books and by attending refresher courses during school vacations. He was a convinced Christian and he delighted to share his vision with others. His home was open to the village chil-dren whom he taught and his wife shared her knowledge of home-making with them. The life of the school in all its aspects was something to which they both gave their whole strength and atten-tion. The Ministry of Education valued his creative leadership and, in a time of crisis, the authorities appointed him to a village school in a very isolated part of Equatoria Province, among a people who were not of his own tribe. He went gladly, for he was a fine teacher and he wanted to share his insights with others. A couple of months passed, and rebel soldiers came to the school compound: because he was a government servant they killed him, together with his wife, and threw their bodies into the river.

It would be wrong to give all the credit for peace to the Christians in the Sudan, for others shared in the long search for it, including many of the northern leaders. Nevertheless it is clear that, when historians finally write the history of that long struggle, they will recognize the loyalty of many Christians to the search for brother-hood, implicit in the Lord's prayer, as one of the important factors leading to its peaceful conclusion.[19]

These few examples taken from a single country show the practical results which can flow from the recognition of brotherhood created by a faithful and responsible use of the Lord's prayer. Every reader will have examples to add from his or her own experience: some will be private to themselves or about some of the very many humble and anonymous people who practise neighbourliness or who operate CARE schemes and the like. (Just as I write this, I notice through the window a party of Rangers who have brought handicapped girls in wheel-chairs on a visit to our cathedral.) Others will be taken from the stories of contemporary heroes of the Christian church, people like Dietrich Bonhoeffer who 'built bridges' from within Hitler's Germany, Martin Luther King who dreamed his great dream, or

Mother Theresa who 'does something beautiful for God' in Calcutta.

In the contemporary world, there are many opportunities for Christians to take the initiative in building bridges between the nations, and between different groups in particular societies. Many are called to do this at great cost to themselves, like those who serve in community projects like Corymeela in Northern Ireland or in the inner city areas of large conurbations. In South Africa, *apartheid* divides human people into separate groups on irrational grounds, and its effect is to deny human rights and human dignity to the majority of those who live and work in that country. Because the pitiless power of a strong government seeks to enforce *apartheid*, it is a costly, wearisome task to go on working for a just, multi-racial society, and for its achievement by peaceful, non-violent means. All honour, therefore, to the leaders of the South African Council of Churches who, at great cost to themselves, maintain the witness of the gospel to the fundamental unity of all mankind.

The witness given by Dr Beyers Naudé, Director of the Christian Institute, at his trial in South Africa in 1973, is a courageous example of the Christian cause.

Many of the convictions which had become clearer to me during my previous years of theological study now crystallized. Firstly, I discovered that the truth of the Bible conveyed to us clearly that God created all the nations of the world in one blood and . . . that the unity of the human race is fundamental for the calling of man on earth . . . Secondly this theological study brought me to the conviction that the Church of Christ is one – Jesus Christ founded his Church, his one Church here on earth, and nowhere in the New Testament is there any ground for the existence of different separate fragmented church communities . . . In the third place I discovered that the Church . . . has a definite calling and responsibility to witness in every sphere of human life, not only in the personal but also in the social sphere, political, economic, education, yes, every aspect. And in the fourth place it became clearer to me than ever before that the central message of the Gospel and the central task and responsibility of the Christian on earth is to act in the name of God as reconciler between those who live in tension, in hatred and bitterness over against each other.[20]

These are insights which Christians have to offer to our contemporary world and for which they must stand up and be counted. They are of particular importance at a time when so many divisive factors hinder the emergence of true community between nations and ethnic groups.

5 Young Prince of Glory

God was in Christ

At the centre of the church's witness to God's grace is the great mystery of the passion, death and resurrection of Jesus Christ. The events of that single week within the long span of human history cluster together as integral parts of one great drama, and they are commemorated in the furnishings at the centre of almost all church buildings, the communion table and the crucifix or cross. This emphasis upon the passion goes back to the earliest days of the church, and the gospels demonstrate its importance by the amount of space they give to its story. St Paul was determined to focus 'the attested truth of God' on the story of 'Jesus nailed to the cross', and he told that story to such effect that Jesus Christ 'was openly displayed upon his cross' to people who had never been near Palestine.[1]

At first sight the story of Calvary is like the stories of other human beings who have struggled with disappointment and frustration, or whose leadership has been rejected by those they have tried to serve. The prophets were tragic figures of this kind in the Old Testament, and there have been many others in the histories of the nations. Not all have died by so cruel a death as crucifixion, but they have all tasted the same bitterness of rejection.

Yet, in a strange way, the story of Jesus is different from those which might be compared with it. Certain features make it unique, even as a human story.

First, the suffering of Jesus was totally undeserved. He had given himself generously and unsparingly to his ministry of teaching and healing. Without a home of his own, he had travelled throughout Galilee and beyond, teaching the multitudes who thronged and jostled him, healing the many who were brought to him: the pressures upon him forced him to seek opportunities for prayer through the night or in the early morning, yet he stopped his disciples from hindering mothers who brought their babies to him for blessing.

Secondly, he bore himself throughout the days of his passion and crucifixion without a trace of self-pity or of resentment towards his enemies. He kept his attention on the needs of those who were close to him; Peter, his mother, even Judas, Pilate and the dying thief, and he prayed for the forgiveness of his executioners.

Thirdly, there is a strange but marked contrast between the use of God's power which Jesus exercised on behalf of others in acts of healing, and his own helplessness when caught up as a victim in the evil purposes of others. Jesus did nothing to claim divine aid against the scheming of the Jewish authorities, or to force Pilate to change his mind. In the Upper Room, he tried to dissuade Judas, but only by the gentleness of courtesy and love. There is a helplessness about Jesus which is nevertheless both dignified and strong.

Fourthly, Jesus experienced a strong inner tension which showed itself in a 'deep agitation of spirit'.[2] This 'storm-tossing' (to translate the Greek literally), was in some ways private to Jesus, and it was far beyond the ability of the disciples to help him. This inner tension showed itself not only in Jesus' words at the supper table, but above all as he prayed in the Garden of Gethsemane, and uttered the strange cry on the cross, 'My God, my God, why hast thou forsaken me?' Yet, at the last, the tension was relieved and the Lord Christ commended himself to God in the habitual trust of his daily prayers, 'Father, into thy hands I commit my spirit'.[3]

Fifthly, although the passion proper began on Palm Sunday and lasted only till Easter Day, it cast its shadow a long way behind, almost to the beginning of Christ's ministry. In the temptation, he committed himself to a course of action which would inevitably lead to conflict with the aspirations of his own people: the glories of a temporal kingdom were not for him. At an early stage in his ministry he began to warn his disciples that he might be taken from them and he responded to Peter's recognition of his God-given mission by talking about suffering and rejection.[4] Although scholars differ about the details, the evidence suggests that Jesus interpreted his God-given mission according to the example of prophets like Jeremiah who had suffered pain, injustice and humiliation in order to rescue their people from disaster, 'bearing the penalty of their guilt'. This understanding of prophethood (as interpreted in the second part of Isaiah) probably provided the model which guided Jesus in working out what it meant to be God's servant. From his baptism onwards, Jesus accepted the principle of vicarious suffering, i.e. suffering undertaken on behalf of, or instead of, another, as his destiny, even if at the beginning he expected that others would share it with him.[5]

These five factors taken together suggest that the passion and death of Christ were directly linked with the purposes of God. The story is tragic because the suffering was wholly undeserved, and it is marked by a calm dignity because of the conduct and bearing of Jesus, but its significance is much greater. It is an action which is closely related to the purposes of God: it is not just a human story, but a great drama in which God is directly involved.

The apostles wrestled with the problem of explaining the *rationale* of the passion and resurrection of their Lord, and they used a variety of explanations to show how these events were related to the will of God.

These explanations are valuable and, because of their apostolic authority, they must be taken with the utmost seriousness. They are the foundation of Christian teaching and preaching.[6] Nevertheless, in the end, they all come back to the basic affirmation made by St Paul that 'God was in Christ reconciling the world to himself' (2 Cor. 5.19). Through his servant Jesus, God engaged with the forces of evil, and revealed how he, the gracious God, reacts to hostility, violence and aggression. I find an entry in David Livingstone's diary a particular help in this respect: it is dated 30 July 1872, only a few months before his death.

> What is the atonement of Christ? It is himself. It is the inherent and everlasting mercy of God made apparent to human eyes and ears. The everlasting love was disclosed by our Lord's life and death. It showed that God forgives because He loves to forgive. He works by smiles if possible; if not, by frowns. Pain is only a means of enforcing love.[7]

In ancient Greek plays, the confusion of relationships and conflict of duties which made up the drama of a particular tragedy sometimes produced too great a tangle for the playwright to resolve on the human plane. He might then resort to a theatrical device whereby an actor representing one of the gods appeared in a balcony above the stage and spoke to the actors beneath. This *deus ex machina* or 'contrived deity', would thereby resolve the tangle and bring the tragedy to a tidy ending. The Lord Christ, however, is no *deus ex machina* speaking from the security of a balcony. He himself walked the road of life, became stained with its dust and tired with its strife, shouldered its pains and frustrations, suffered its humiliation, its alienation, and its loneliness: he was totally involved in the great drama of human life.

He was also, however, the Word of God, and in him God was reconciling the world unto himself. His death, as well as his life, was a revelation of the Eternal God, and he revealed him as the one who bears the burden of evil and thereby deprives it of its power to hurt and destroy. The selfless, persevering, gentle love which Jesus showed to his contemporaries in Gethsemane and at Calvary was a translation of the grace of God into the terms of a human life. The love of Jesus for Peter and the others makes it possible for you and me to be certain that the eternal Father comes running down the road to meet us, and that he searches for us continually. John of Patmos expressed a true insight when he saw Jesus standing 'in the very middle of the throne (of God) . . . with the marks of Calvary upon him'.[8] For the love of God is the love of Calvary which is for every bearing hurt and sorrow and pain, and seeking through it the renewal of his creation.

Here, then, is the heart of Christian belief about God. In its simplest terms, it is the conviction that the eternal God perseveres in love for his creation, and carries in himself the pain and disappointment caused by failure on the part of his creatures. This suffering he carries in himself without repudiating or rejecting the creatures who cause it. To believe this of God gives us the confidence to believe that God has not tired of his creation, despite the disappointments and failures of his creatures. Graciously and in his own sovereign way he still works hopefully for the fulfilment of his purposes and the building of his new Jerusalem.

This suffering-in-love, however, is not confined to the human scene, but is an integral element in the whole creative process. There is a mystery in the divine passion which is beyond our capacity to understand or to express. It is hidden in the inner being of God and expressed in the darkness of Calvary which we cannot penetrate.

> But none of the ransomed ever knew
> How dark were the waters crossed,
> Or how dark was the night that the Lord passed through,
> To find his sheep that was lost.

The cross is more than an episode in time related to the needs of human people alone. It is a revelation in human terms, for those who have the will to understand it, of the dynamics of divine love. It helps us not only to understand the human adventure, but the long processes of creation as well.

To people of other religious faiths, Christianity often appears to be a religion which emphasizes overmuch the problem of evil and personal experiences of sin and forgiveness. Thus it was once my privilege, when a student at Canterbury, to entertain a devout Muslim friend in our home. I took him to holy communion in the college chapel and later to evensong in the cathedral. He seemed to appreciate much of the worship, but his main comment was to say how puzzled he was by our apparent hang-up over sin and forgiveness. He had been puzzled by the familiar Anglican pattern of exhortation, confession, and absolution at both the services which he attended with me.

Islam lays much stress upon God's sovereignty and teaches the transcendence of God clearly and without compromise. Islam also teaches that God is compassionate and forgiving, and that his mercy is extended to his creatures: 'his mercy and knowledge encompass all things'. Muslims are taught to trust themselves to his mercy and to seek refuge with God from the power of evil. The last two chapters of the Qur'an, for example, are often used as prayers to avert the attacks of evil, and to give protection against spells, jealousy and the suggestion of evil thoughts.[9]

But although God is known as 'the Compassionate, the Merciful', Muslims do not include mercy and compassion among the seven essential attributes of God. These are concerned with his sovereignty alone: God lives eternally, without beginning and ending; he knows all things: he can do all things; all things exist by his will; he hears all things; he sees all things; he reveals himself to men. God's mercy is like the mercy of a potentate which is exercised when he chooses to do so. 'Whoever God wishes to guide aright, he opens his breast to (receive) Islam, and who ever he wishes to lead astray he makes his breast narrow and contracted, as if he were trying to climb up into heaven: so God lays abomination upon those who do not believe.'[10]

It is not surprising, in view of this emphasis upon the sovereignty of God, that Islam rejects not only the incarnation but the Christian story of the cross as well. The Qur'an itself does not give much attention to the passion of Christ, and there are only a few references in it to his death, some of which are difficult to interpret and slightly ambiguous. There is, however, one explicit denial of the crucifixion which shows how far the Qur'an is from an understanding of

Christian belief about the self-giving nature of God's love. This denial occurs in a passage which rebukes the Jews for various acts of unbelief, and it refers only in passing to the crucifixion.

> Because they (the Jews) break their covenant, and disbelieve in the signs of God, and kill the prophets without just cause . . . and because they say, 'We killed the Messiah, Jesus the son of Mary, the Apostle of God';
> (they did not kill him, nor did they crucify him, but a resemblance was made for them; those who dispute about it are in doubt about it [or him]; they have no certain knowledge about it, but only follow conjecture; they did not kill him certainly, but God raised him to himself; God is mighty and wise. There is no one of the People of the Book but will believe in him before his death, and, on the Day of Resurrection, he will be a witness against them.)
> and because of the wrong-doing of those who Judaize . . . and because they devour the wealth of the people with what is worthless; We [i.e. God] have prepared for the unbelievers among them a painful punishment.[11]

The Arabic commentators disagree about the exact interpretation of these verses from the Qur'an but they agree on one significant point. They all affirm that God in his sovereign power extricated Jesus from the plots of the Jews and raised him directly to heaven. He did this either by allowing someone (Judas, a thirteenth apostle, a bystander?) to be crucified in Jesus' place by mistake, or by rescuing him from the cross before or at the moment of death. However he achieved it, God refused to allow his servant to die at the hands of the Jews and, instead, demonstrated his sovereignty by raising Jesus to heaven. (Many Muslim traditions, as well as popular Muslim teaching, say that Jesus will return to earth at an unknown date in the future, when the Hour of Judgment comes near, in order to die a natural death and so fulfil references in the Qur'an to his death.)[12]

The Qur'anic attitude towards the story of the crucifixion reflects the experience of the prophet Muhammad. During the first years of his ministry in his home town of Mecca, he and his followers suffered indignity and persecution on account of his preaching. At this period his ministry was very similar to that of some of the Old Testament prophets. Then came the Hijra, the deliberate transfer of Muslim authority to Medina, a town some three hundred miles to the north of Mecca. The Arab townsfolk there accepted Muhammad as God's apostle, and recognized his authority to arbitrate in their disputes: he consolidated his position, and in ten short years brought most of Arabia under his authority. His authority was based on his position and work as God's apostle, but it was strengthened and maintained by military campaigns and expeditions, by the imposition of taxation, and by the exercise of secular authority. Muhammad was sincere in attributing this success to the will and support of God, for he saw himself as God's appointed servant and representative: God in his sovereign power would always in the end secure the triumph and vindication of his servants. A similar pattern of initial rejection and final triumph, with judgment executed on their enemies, underlies the stories of all the great prophets as they are told in the Qur'an.

Islam and Christianity share many beliefs in common, not least belief in one living personal God to whom all human persons must one day give account of their stewardship: they share many of the prophets, and they follow patterns of prayer which are similar to each other at many significant points. But there is one fundamental difference between them. Islam sets the sovereign authority of God over against the sinfulness of men: God circumvents evil by his power, and he brings his purposes to fruition by exercising his authority. In the end his will triumphs, by confounding the evil doer and vindicating those who obey him. He forgives, as he chooses, and it is his prerogative to do so. Christianity, on the other hand, believes that God deals with evil by bearing the burden of it himself, and that he defeats it by accepting in himself the hurt and the suffering which it causes in his creation. By accepting it in this way he robs it of its power to destroy and transforms it into good. He demonstrated his way of atonement with final clarity in the passion of Jesus, his Word made man. This is God's way of love and the church is called to bear witness to its truth and its power.

Buddhism is another of the great world religions which attracts the interest and sympathy of many people across the world. It has given much to the human community through its teachings about human destiny, right conduct and self-mastery. In its pure Theravada form, it has no teaching similar to that of Christians about God's encounter with evil: on the contrary, it teaches that, although there is sorrow and suffering in earthly existence, insight and wisdom are the only things which can liberate those who possess them from the sufferings and illusions of earthly existence. This is clearly stated in the first sermon Gautama Buddha preached to his companions after his enlightenment.

> Revered monks, what is the Middle Road that leads to Peace? It is the Noble Eightfold Path, namely, Right Speech, Right Action, Right Livelihood, Right Effort, Right Mindfulness, Right Concentration, Right Views, Right Thought. The Middle Road, revered monks, leads to Peace.

Now, revered monks, this is the Noble Truth as to the origin of sorrow. Earthly existence indeed is sorrowful, decay is sorrowful, disease, death, union with the unpleasing, separation from the pleasing, is sorrowful. The wish which cannot be fulfilled is sorrowful; in brief, to walk the path of desire is sorrowful.

Again, revered monks, this is the Noble Truth as to the origin of sorrow; the recurring desire which is associated with enjoyment and seeks pleasure everywhere, is the cause of this sorrow.

Again, revered monks, this is the Noble Truth as to the cessation of sorrow, and to the acquiring of happiness. It is the cessation of this desiring so that no remnant or trace of it remains. It must be abandoned, renounced, and escaped from.

And once more, revered monks, this is the Noble Truth as to the road which leads to the cessation of sorrow. It is indeed the Noble Eightfold Path.

As soon, revered monks, as my knowledge and insight concerning these Four Noble Truths became complete, I knew that I had attained supreme and full enlightenment. I became aware and fully convinced that my mind was liberated; that existence in its unhappy form had ended; that there would no more be any unhappy survival.[13]

Thus Buddhism teaches that deliverance from suffering and from evil is not the gift of God but a conquest won by man's intellect and will on his own responsibility. Man must work out his own salvation by his own efforts. 'By oneself evil is done, by oneself one is defiled. By oneself evil is left undone, by oneself alone one is purified. Purity and impurity depend on oneself. No one purifies another.'[14] Walking the Eightfold Path leads to insight and wisdom which dispel ignorance, desire and sorrow. Its fruit is serenity, knowledge, and enlightenment which is *nirvana* – the state of perfect peace and bliss.

These short discussions of the teachings of Islam and Buddhism about the mercy of God and the mastery of evil demonstrate the uniqueness of Christianity. Christianity is not just another example of a common religious attitude towards life, or of the worship which human people offer to the Eternal Being whose power is shown in creation and in providence. Christianity is not just another version of the ancient monotheistic faith of the Middle East, which is expressed in its most absolute terms in Islam. Nor does Christianity, like orthodox Buddhism, offer a way of self-mastery and purification by which the religious person tames the desires of life and attains serenity. At the centre of Christianity is something different, and, among all the religions, unique. This is the belief that the Eternal God revealed himself, in the person of Jesus of Nazareth, to be one with

53

humanity in their age-long struggle with the forces of evil, and that he masters them on their behalf. This deliverance is the act of God and an unmerited gift to mankind made on the basis of grace alone. This is the gospel which the church is commissioned to proclaim.

The new creation

The dignity, happiness and well-being of human existence are threatened by the disrupting forces of evil. Jealousy and resentment break up friendships and destroy the harmony of families, self-centredness prevents parents or guardians from giving adequate care to their children, and when it is present in either young or old it alienates them from each other. In the wider groupings of society, avarice, greed and self-centred ambition cause strife and confrontation within places of work and in local communities. In very many areas across the world, social injustice of various kinds deprives people of the just fruits of their labours, and of those basic human rights which people need to enjoy if they are to live truly human lives. The result is often violence, or escape into the fantasy world of drugs and deviation, or hopelessness. Moreover, evil is not just a fact to be reckoned with in the structures of society: it is present also within the individual psyche and often causes loneliness, alienation, aggression or neurosis. All of us know, within ourselves, the potent power of evil to rob us of well-being and to arouse attitudes and reactions which make us feel ashamed.

There are, I realize, many questions which might be asked about the presence of evil in the universe and its relation to the will and purpose of God, or about the way evil operates. These questions are important, but they do not affect the reality of its influence in our lives, or of the evil forces which operate in our contemporary world: their influence is plainly seen in every television news broadcast and in our newspapers. For evil, whatever its origin, threatens both our own personal futures, and the search for world community as well. John had good reason for saying about the new Jerusalem of his dreams: 'Nothing unclean shall enter, nor anyone whose ways are false or foul.' [15]

We imagine that evil's hold on us is too strong to be shaken off, but Christ in his passion demonstrated that love is stronger than hatred and evil. He gives us, as his disciples, the hope of victory over evil and the courage to stand and fight against it. Similarly, although we are tempted to believe that evil has the last word, and that death

54

and frustration will overwhelm us and all our endeavours, the resurrection of Christ, his coming to life again in the glory and vitality of God, assures us that the ultimate victory is with God and with his children. 'Do not be afraid', Christ says. 'I am the first and the last, and I am the living one; for I was dead and now I am alive for evermore, and I hold the keys of Death and Death's domain' (Rev. 1.17–18). The passion and resurrection of Christ, when shared with others, have power to renew love, and hope and goodness, and to give his disciples victory over evil and over death.

St Paul summed up the significance of the liberation which Christ has won for the Christian by saying: 'when anyone is united to Christ, there is a new act of creation; the old order has gone, and a new order has begun'. This, however, is not significant just for the Christian individual alone: it has significance for the rest of humanity as well. So St James called Christians 'the first fruits of God's creatures', and John of Patmos used the phrase 'first-fruits of humanity'.[16] Christians are, or should be, the pioneers of the new humanity which God is bringing into being through Christ, for they are already experiencing in themselves the renewal which God intends for all his creation. Christ is not only 'the first-born among a large family of brothers', but he is also in relation to mankind as a whole 'the second Adam'.[17] In Christ, God made a new and fresh beginning and its success is assured by the victory which Christ, 'the second Adam', achieved over evil. Those who are inspired by his spirit and live in his way are the prototype of a new re-ordered humanity. They are 'born again' to become God's true children living out in the human community as a whole the pattern of life which God means all mankind to enjoy. With them is the promise of the future; they stand at the gates of the new Jerusalem, and invite others to enter it with them.

The church celebrates this gift of new creation in the service of the holy communion. Jesus celebrated his last supper with his disciples on the eve of his passion, and it was marked by the exit of the traitor and the sense of impending disaster. But Jesus saw beyond his passion to the coming reign of God: he made bread and wine the pledges of his victory and by sharing them with his disciples strengthened their faith. After the resurrection, they continued to recognize his presence with them in their fellowship, and they made their common meals foretastes of the heavenly banquet. When Christians meet in fellowship at the holy communion they share together in a fellowship which transcends all natural divisions, they celebrate the great acts of

Christ, and they meet with him 'who was dead and is alive for evermore'. They look forward with joy to God's tomorrow.

The way of love

The church is the 'Body of Christ', called to serve and to minister in the world as Jesus had done during his earthly life (1 Cor. 12.27ff.). Its members are called, as the prototype of a re-ordered humanity, to demonstrate the way of love which Jesus taught his disciples was to be the pattern of their behaviour. Thus the apostles who had been apprenticed to Jesus in Galilee took great pains, after the resurrection, to explain his way, or life-style, to those who became members of the churches which they founded. Indeed they placed so strong an emphasis on this practical aspect of their teaching that the first communities of Christians were known as 'followers of the way'.[18] Their letters, in the New Testament, help us to understand what was meant by 'the way', and to reconstruct an outline of the basic teaching which they gave throughout the scattered churches. In particular, they paid attention to the relationships which ought to exist between husbands and wives, between parents and children, between employers and employees and, in an elementary form, between citizens and government.[19]

At the centre of the apostles' teaching were the two commandments which Jesus said summed up the whole Law, namely, to love God with one's whole personality, and to love one's neighbour as oneself. At the same time, they interpreted love as Christ had defined it through his ministry and passion, and in accordance with his teaching that the children of God are called to reflect in their own lives the boundless generosity of God, their Father (see chapter 3). Thus they summarized the basic principles of their teaching in statements like the following. 'Be generous to one another, tender-hearted, forgiving one another as God in Christ forgave you. In a word, as God's dear children, try to be like him, and live in love as Christ loved you, and gave himself up on your behalf . . . Be subject to one another out of reverence for Christ' (Eph. 4.32; 5.1–2, 21).

This theme has implications for our personal behaviour, but most readers will be familiar with these and I do not intend to discuss them here. Instead, I wish to set the apostles' teaching in the wider context of social justice and development towards world community. Christians have a responsibility in these fields also to apply the principles of the way of love to which Christ has called them. Perhaps they can be summed up in these words: righteousness, responsibility, restraint, and renewal.

Righteousness The Christian prays for the coming of God's kingdom and the doing of his will on earth as in heaven. God is wholly righteous and, as the Old Testament prophets showed so clearly, religious fervour and observances are no substitute for a commitment to righteousness in the lives of those who worship him (Amos 5.21, 23–4). Righteousness is a central theme in the whole Bible and the churches cannot disregard its claims upon them. No matter what it costs in terms of popularity or of acceptance by others, Christians are called to seek for righteousness in the community. For some this may mean involvement in political struggle and in unpopular causes.

It is true that it is often difficult to establish where right actually lies in this or that particular dispute, for we live in a very complicated society in which rights and privileges conflict with each other. Nor should Christian groups feel that they must become involved in every matter which becomes a subject for public debate. But there are matters in which Christians ought to become involved simply because they pray for the doing of God's will, and it will not be done unless they also are active in seeking for its fulfilment.

Responsibility Like those of other faiths, Christians believe that they are responsible for the use they make of the world and its resources, and the way in which they enable others to share fairly in them. Human people are not proprietors of the world and its resources, they are tenants of planet earth, stewards of its bounty, and responsible to practise careful husbandry. This truth is expressed in the Qur'anic story of Adam, in which God says to the angels, 'I am placing on earth my deputy', i.e. Adam, and then goes on to teach him the names of his creatures, thus putting them within Adam's power.[20]

In the field of personal relationships, the Christian's responsibility is not simply to those in his immediate family or circle of acquaintances. True responsibility, which is a reflection of the way of love, will lead to participation in good neighbour schemes and voluntary social services, to community service of all kinds, and to sensitive decisions in board rooms and planning committees. It will cause senior employees to be generously interested in the welfare of those junior to them, and colleagues to be concerned for one another.

Restraint In the contemporary world, responsibility towards the natural universe is linked with the problems associated with pollution and conservation. Natural resources, of all kinds, are limited in extent and are being exhausted far too rapidly by the affluent nations. This wasteful use of resources threatens the well-being of the whole human community and restraint and moderation are asked of those who are in a position to modify what they take from the world's wealth.

The wasteful use of resources does not only affect the relationship between human people and nature: it affects also relationships between one human community and another. This is particularly true of relationships between the developed Western nations and those of Africa and Asia, as the journalist 'Candidus' pointed out in a recent article.

> When the Prime Minister Mrs Indira Gandhi opened an Indian national conference on population a few days before the end of 1974 she rounded on Western countries for lecturing India on priorities – as between agriculture, industry and nuclear development, for example – while 'a tiny majority in the affluent countries is using up food, petrol and other essential commodities out of all proportion to their needs'. She had been told she said, that more milk powder was fed to animals in Western Europe than went to the children of all the developing countries put together ...
>
> Looking back at the last quarter of a century, it is difficult not to reach the conclusion that some kind of short-sighted, selfish madness had gripped the developed world. Year after year the aim was 'growth' – the national product must be increased 5, 10, 15, 20%. If you increased it by only one or two per cent you were a failure. This growth, it seemed to be supposed, could go on indefinitely until, presumably, developed countries lived in a gold-plated paradise. No one seemed to consider the flimsy world economic system that allowed us to grow, and few saw the appalling dangers that must inevitably build up as the gulf between the rich and the poor widened.[21]

Christians ought to be in a position to make direct and positive contributions to the adoption of the new attitudes which are needed. They are apprenticed to one who invited his followers to say 'no' to themselves and to find their lives by losing them for the sake of others: who said that 'giving is a happier, more blessed thing, than getting', and who himself had no permanent home or lodging.[22] Many Christians are deeply concerned about issues like these, and seek to adopt a style of life which accepts restraint with joy, and to the enrichment, not the impoverishment of life. Foremost among them are the Bishop of Winchester, John V. Taylor, author of the book *Enough is Enough*,[23] and the Dean of Bristol whose 'Life-Style' movement continues to grow.

It may be, however, that personal self-discipline is not enough and that it must be accompanied by a much more costly and well thought out criticism of the existing structures which make it possible for natural resources to be exploited and excessive profits made by particular groups and individuals. The logic of restraint may lead in the end to a thorough-going socialism, which places the welfare of the whole community above the interests of private individuals, and secures the fulfilment of the individual through his participation in the well-being of his neighbours. This is not to argue for a simple equation of Christian restraint with the policies of parties which claim the title 'socialist', but to plead for a Christian socialism which takes seriously the need for restraint upon individual interests in order to safeguard the welfare of the whole community. Moreover, in such an interdependent world as that of the twentieth century, the community must be defined in global and universal, as much as in national, terms.

Renewal The Christian community is set in the world to bear witness to the possibility of renewal. This is perhaps the most significant of Christian contributions because it grows directly out of the Christian's understanding and experience of the resurrection of Christ. In all kinds of ways, as we explored in the previous section, the Christian gospel gives the promise that failure and defeat may be transformed into victory and a means of renewal. The promise of forgiveness and acceptance is assured in the reconciling love of God made effective at Calvary, and received in response to the Christian gospel. Hope for better achievements in the future, and the promise of eventual victory, are guaranteed by the resurrection and by the resources of the Holy Spirit made available to those who open their lives to receive them. These are the grounds for Christian optimism, and elements in the good news which Christians are called to share with others. The human community needs this kind of renewal if its peoples are to achieve those other goals which are so important: social justice, mutual responsibility and restraint.

6 Resources of Power

Divine energy and human living

In chapter 1 of this book we explored some of the pressures which crowd in upon us who live in the twentieth century. Clearly if we are to realize any of the dreams for world community which we explored in chapter 2 we need deep inner resources of the spirit to enable us to cope with the challenges and opportunities of our times.

These resources are available – the divine Spirit, which all through the ages has been at work in God's creation, presiding over the long processes of its development. Like the rocket thrusts given to correct the course of a space ship, his influence has nudged the processes of evolution in this or that direction so that at long last the biosphere came into being on planet earth and with it the possibilities of conscious personal life. Since man came into being in the last stage of earth's 4,500 million year history,[1] the divine Spirit has guided human people in their efforts to build just and good societies, and his influence is discernible at many points.

Christians associate the Spirit in a special way with Jesus Christ, and they believe that his influence is active among his disciples. The Holy Spirit inspires them to become the kind of people that Jesus was himself – people who master life with hope, courage and confidence nourished by their trust in God. The Holy Spirit was given communally to the apostles and their associates but, at the same time, he was believed to reside in the personalities of individual believers and St Paul went so far as to say: 'if a man does not possess the Spirit of Christ, he is no Christian'.[2]

It may seem a strange concept to speak of a human personality indwelt by the spirit of another, even in the context of religious experience, but there are many analogies in ordinary human living. We often speak, for example, of 'the spirit' of a football team, of an

60

institution or a school, and, as often as not, we associate that 'spirit' with the influence of a particular person such as the captain or headmaster. In marriage also, a husband and wife are influenced by each other in many different ways, not only when they are in each other's presence but also when they are apart. Even when they are separated by long distances, or for a period of days or weeks, each partner is open to the influence of the other and makes responses and decisions in the light of it.

In the Old Testament, the Holy Spirit was associated with particular persons who were leaders in the community, as generals, statesmen, prophets or master craftsmen. But the prophets looked forward to a time when the Spirit of God would 'be poured out on all mankind . . . even upon slaves and slave-girls'. The apostles believed that this promise was fulfilled on the day of Pentecost and it is clear from what they wrote that they expected every Christian to be influenced by the Holy Spirit. Thus they could move easily between thinking of the whole church as the great temple 'built into a spiritual dwelling for God', and the thought that the personality of each individual Christian is 'a shrine of the indwelling Holy Spirit: and the Spirit is God's gift to you'.[3] Again we need to remember that Christians are called to be light to the world: their experience of the Holy Spirit is not for their own exclusive use or enjoyment, but intended to help the whole human community recognize the presence of the Holy Spirit active throughout human history, and to respond to his influence.

Sometimes a false distinction is made between activities which are obviously religious, such as prayer, worship, and other church-centred activities, and the ordinary activities of everyday life which, by contrast are called 'worldly' or 'secular'. This is to misunderstand what the scriptures say about the Holy Spirit. Not only is the Spirit associated in them with the act of creation but, even more explicitly, he was believed to have inspired the heroes of the Old Testament to perform exploits in the hurly-burly of their everyday political and social life. The craftsmen who built the Tabernacle were believed to have been inspired by the Spirit for their work, and David to compose songs and music. He inspired Saul to accomplish a great feat of military heroism, and the qualities needed by an efficient and just administrator were in his gift. He inspired the prophets to preach sermons which were directly relevant to the political problems of their times. There is, as we shall see, a different emphasis in the way the apostles thought of his influence, but it was still directed towards the actual social environment in which Christians were called to live and to witness.[4]

Among the gifts of the Spirit which are mentioned in the New Testament are the gifts of healing and of 'ecstatic utterance'. They are not the only gifts of the Spirit, and there is no evidence in the New Testament that they are given to every, or even to most Christians. Personally, I include the work of the caring and medical professions within the healing work of the Spirit of God, and I believe that those who have the gift of 'ecstatic utterance' should use it with the greatest care. They are signs of the Holy Spirit's activity, but not the only ones, nor the most important.

The Holy Spirit works in and through human personalities and it sometimes happens that natural excitement and enthusiasm take charge rather than the Holy Spirit. The more important gifts are those which inspire people to act with wisdom, to express truth clearly and simply, to sustain faith and courage, to accept responsibility, to care adequately for others and above all to love.[5]

Clearing away these misconceptions helps us to see more clearly why the Holy Spirit was given to human people, to dwell within their personalities and to inspire them. It was to make them truly human by drawing them up into the great creative activity of God, and to make them effective agents of his purpose in the world of everyday happenings. Perhaps that can be expressed by saying that the Spirit of Jesus is given to his disciples to make them, in reality as well as in name, the prototype of that new humanity of which he is the (second) Adam. (See above, pages 55f.)

Water, wind and fire

Let us reflect for a moment on the power of water to nourish and sustain life. When we lived in Amman, the capital of the Kingdom of Jordan, we used to go for picnics to a valley in the hills of Gilead to the north of the city. The hills which enclosed the valley were bare and barren and the crops upon them thin and scanty. In the heat of a summer's day it was no pleasure to walk across them or even to stop the car. The valley, however, was different. At its head great springs of water gushed out from the hillside, and filled a wide pool from which the village people drew their water. We always noticed the contrast between the lonely road across the hills down to the valley, and the hustle and bustle which confused us as we neared the water.

The waters fed a stream which wound its way westward some twenty miles to the Jordan river. Small farms, orchards, and gardens lay along its banks and it was our enjoyment to walk down the valley road and to picnic somewhere in the shade of a tree by the side of the stream. All along the road one noticed the contrast between the living valley and the barren hillside above it. At different spots along the valley there would be a patch of green on the hillside marking a place where water oozed out of the rocks. The same pattern is to be seen in the wilder parts of Britain, in the Scottish Highlands, for example, or on Exmoor. The provision of piped water has made us less sensitive to the presence of water in urban areas or in the milder parts of south-east England, but even there archaeological research often locates the old centres of villages and hamlets where there is a supply of fresh water. The Anglo-Saxon and Danish settlers who founded them had a good eye for sources of water.

Such is the background to the great invitation of Jesus, when he 'stood and cried aloud, "If anyone is thirsty let him come to me; whoever believes in me, let him drink." As Scripture says, "Streams of living water shall flow out from within him"' (John 7.37–9). To be indwelt by the Spirit of God is to have within oneself a source of vitality which constantly revives and refreshes the inner springs of our personalities.

I have begun with the image of water because that speaks to me personally in a fresh and vivid way: I once had charge of a community in Africa where the supply of water was a constant preoccupation. From the beginning, however, the Spirit of God was pictured as a wind which blew from God to touch and to move human beings. (Both in Hebrew and Greek the same words are used for 'wind' and for 'spirit'.) It was a natural metaphor to use when explaining how men like Saul were suddenly impelled to do great deeds: the wind of God blew upon them and no one saw from where it had come or where it went. In a more general way the wind of God touched everyone, for 'the Lord God formed (a) man from the dust of the ground and breathed into his nostrils the breath of life' (Gen. 2.7).

Stand on a headland on a summer's day and watch the sailing boats becalmed and drifting with the current, their sails flapping idly against their masts. A breeze springs up and the boats now run before the wind, their sails set and braced for movement. The branches of trees and bushes are set dancing, and the corn waves in the wind. We all know the power of the wind: it brings with it clouds, rain and snow; it dries the washing and searches out rubbish in the corners of our yards, it lifts dustbin lids, and blows down leaves. To be touched by God's wind is to be moved to action, to be stirred and shaken.

Fire is another word associated with the Spirit: 'there appeared to them tongues like flames of fire'. In olden times, fire was the great refiner and purifier. It was used both to refine precious metals, and to consume rubbish: (the town rubbish heaps outside Jerusalem in the Valley of Hinnom gave their name to the Jewish version of Hell, Gehenna). We still use the same processes, in modern chemical processes and in our incinerators.

Another prime function of fire is to serve as a source of energy. Perhaps we are more familiar with this than people were in past ages, for we have harnessed fire to produce energy in power stations, in the engine rooms of ships, or in the turbines of jet aircraft. Ancient peoples feared the destructive power of fire when it razed crops or destroyed the crowded quarters of cities by accident or in war. Even so, like us, they felt the strange power of fire, burning in the hearth of a home, to give the whole family a sense of vitality and of well-being. Those who know the fire of God's Spirit are in touch with a source of energy which makes all things possible.

The apostles in their letters describe the ways in which Christians experienced the influence of the Holy Spirit in terms of the expectations and attitudes of daily life. Thus, for example, the Holy Spirit gives a deep inner strength to those who are influenced and inspired by him: they possess resources which stand the strains and pressures of life and enable them to cope with them. So St Paul prayed for his friends to the Father, 'that out of the treasures of his glory he may grant you strength and power through his Spirit in your inner being' (Eph. 3.16).

Again the influence of the Holy Spirit shows itself in qualities of character which are very like those of Jesus: 'love, joy, peace, patience, kindness, goodness, fidelity, gentleness, and self-control' (Gal. 5.22–3). People with characters like that have resources which can help them master any set of circumstances: love gives them generosity to care unselfishly for others, joy keeps them cheerful and hopeful in times of difficulty, peace gives them mastery of anxiety and fear. They are people whose characters are refreshed by the water of the Spirit and warmed by his fire.

The effectiveness of the Spirit in moving people to action and commitment was demonstrated in the book of the Acts of the Apostles. In that story the Spirit moved the apostles to new enterprises of mission – among the synagogues of Jerusalem, on the desert highway, in the great city of Antioch, in the sea-ports of Roman Asia. In this the promise of Jesus was fulfilled that 'they would receive power when the Holy Spirit came upon them, and bear witness for him to the ends of the earth'.[6] Moreover, it was the Holy Spirit who promoted the growth and development of their communities. He created fellowship between their members and endowed each individual with a particular gift which was of value to the whole. 'There are varieties of gifts, but the same Spirit . . . In each of us the Spirit is manifested in one particular way, for some useful purpose' (1 Cor. 12.4, 7). The Greek word for 'gifts', *charismata*, is associated with grace (*charis*), and means a gift given freely and of grace. It emphasizes that, although the gifts of the Spirit are often linked with natural capabilities, they are also special endowments given by God in order to achieve his purposes.

Unfailing optimism

Cardinal Suenens concludes his great book about the Holy Spirit with a prayer which ends in these words:

> Give your hope to me and to all your Church,
> that the Church today may bear witness to the world,
> that the world may know all Christians by their look of
> joy and serenity,
> their warm and generous hearts,
> and the unfailing optimism which rises from God's
> secret, everlasting spring of joyful hope.[7]

As we noted above, pages 7f., we live in times of crisis when people feel themselves to be under pressure for all kinds of reasons. In 1975, the Archbishops' Call to the Nation drew attention to the serious state of affairs and the Archbishop of Canterbury, at a press conference, stated his intentions in these words: 'I want to speak not only to members of the churches but to all those who are concerned for the welfare of our nation at a time when many thoughtful people feel that we are drifting towards chaos.' A few weeks later the British Council of Churches went further and declared at their Third Assembly: 'The mood of the nation is a sombre one. The picture is of insecurity and anxiety verging on fear, disillusionment and tiredness bordering on hopelessness, perplexity and bewilderment leading to a sense of powerlessness.'[8] Such an assessment of general attitudes is echoed in many current analyses of the present situation, both in print and on television. Nor is the sense of crisis present in Britain alone: as we saw in earlier chapters it is common elsewhere as well.

It is against this background that Christians are called to be people of optimism and of hope. They have good grounds for hope for they believe in the living God. Like the Old Testament prophet who preached during the siege of Jerusalem when the future of that city looked very dark and disaster threatened, they bear witness to him and declare:

> The Lord, he is God for real,
> God alive,
> King for ever,
> (Jer. 10.10 my translation)

This hope is founded on the confidence that God has not abandoned his purpose for humanity, to which he set his hand in the long process of creation and which he re-affirmed in the incarnation of his Son. God is personally and intimately involved in the human enterprise and he will not give up in despair.

Christians express their hope in several different ways. *First*, in the conviction that all things are held together in the will and purpose of God and that there is an underlying direction and coherence within the human enterprise. No human person can understand the whole of God's purpose, but we see enough to catch glimpses of the underlying scheme of things and thus to go on in hope. Moreover the Christian believes that the divine purpose is a gracious one which seeks the well-being of the whole created universe. To this we bear witness in the first confession of our baptism: 'I believe and trust in God the Father who made the world.' (See above, chapter 4.)

Secondly, the Christian knows that in the passion of Christ and in responding to it there is the possibility of renewal. There can be no final defeat either for himself or the human community. Christ's selfless love transforms evil into good and, by forgiving and accepting them, liberates its agents from its power. Moreover, the passion of Christ on Calvary is one with the graciousness of God the Creator who renews his creation by bearing in himself the contradictions of evil. These insights are given in a Christian's personal experience of the forgiveness and generosity of Christ and they give him ground for hope. The second confession of our baptism bears witness to this hope of victory: 'I believe and trust in his Son Jesus Christ who redeemed mankind.' (See above, chapter 5.)

Thirdly, the Christian is hopeful because he knows that, although the resources of God's eternal Spirit are dispersed and active throughout the universe, they are also available to those who respond to him in trust and worship. The Spirit of God, the wind and fire of God, is active in the human community, moving people to seek his will and giving them energy to achieve it. Although acting sometimes with dramatic force and suddenness, the Spirit more commonly operates like a spring of sweet water deep within human personalities, enriching their characters and developing his gifts of courage and perseverance, peace, joy and love. The hope of the Christian lies in the knowledge that he and others may depend on the resources of the Holy Spirit. So the Christian makes the third confession at his baptism: 'I believe and trust in his Holy Spirit who sanctifies the people of God.'

Secrets of success

The best summary of Jesus' teaching about the way in which people should live as the children of God in his world is found in the so-called Beatitudes at the beginning of St Matthews's account of The Sermon on the Mount (Matt. 5.1–10). They will help us to draw together the different facets of the gospel which we have discussed together in the last three chapters of this book. In their simple form they are as follows:

How blest are those who know their need of God; the kingdom of
    Heaven is theirs.
How blest are the sorrowful; they shall find consolation.
How blest are those of a gentle spirit; they shall have the earth for
    their possession.
How blest are those who hunger and thirst to see right prevail;
    they shall be satisfied.
How blest are those who show mercy; mercy shall be shown to
    them.
How blest are those whose hearts are pure; they shall see God.
How blest are the peacemakers; God shall call them his sons.
How blest are those who have suffered persecution for the cause of
    right; the kingdom of Heaven is theirs.

As a young man, I was inclined to dismiss these sayings as a rather pious, other-worldly code of ethics: the title, 'the Beatitudes', and the old translation obscured their real importance. This misunderstanding was, however, corrected for me in East Berlin during the winter of 1949 when I met a group of young Christians meeting for Bible study in the Russian controlled sector of the city. They were in chapel, and they finished their prayers by chanting, in a kind of dialogue style with their leader, what sounded to me like a battle hymn, stirring them to action. I do not know German and did not realize until afterwards that they were in fact reciting the Beatitudes together. Later discussion made it clear that they made this passage the basis for their discipleship and for their witness in the dangerous and taxing situation in which they lived.

Since that time I have seen the Beatitudes in a new light. Indeed I would prefer to call the passage by such a title as 'True Success', for that is the implication of the word 'blessed': it has also a note of joy and gaiety implicit in it. They are very simple sayings but they are full of wisdom and they sum up the teaching of Jesus in clear but profound statements about the real dignity and meaning of human existence.

The truly successful person, Jesus says, *is the one who lives in dependence upon God*, the Ground of all Being, and the Creator and Sustainer of the universe: believing that God reigns and that he is gracious, the believer is in a position to receive and to use the resources of God's kingdom. By responding to God in trust and in worship, he becomes open to the influence and strengthening of his Spirit.

The truly successful person is open and sensitive to others, both in their sorrows and their joys: walking the way of love, he builds community, and finds strengthening for his own life in loving relationships with others.

The truly successful person is content to wait for God's purposes to mature, and for others to make their own responses to God's truth: he believes that God is always active within his creation, and seeks by understanding and patience to work within God's gracious purposes. Working with God, and waiting for God's time, he builds securely and achieves his aims. He rejoices to have a share in God's new Jerusalem.

The truly successful person commits himself and his resources to the pursuit of righteousness within his community. He accepts the responsibility and restraint which Christ's way asks of his disciples, and takes the message of the gospel out on to the road of life. He knows his efforts to be worthwhile and is confident that victory lies with those who are committed to God's kingdom.

68

The truly successful person is strong enough to be gentle, patient and accepting towards others: forgiving others he himself is forgiven. Knowing that God's goodness has no bounds, he seeks to reflect that goodness in his relationships with others.

The truly successful person masters himself and is whole-hearted in seeking the coming of God's kingdom. He has the assurance of God's presence and his blessing: he rejoices to be part of God's new creation.

The truly successful person gives of himself to make peace, at home or at work, and seeks to promote it in the community. He counts it a privilege to be one of Christ's 'unarmed soldiers of peace': in doing this he reflects the character of God, who is both king and father.

The successful person sacrifices his own interests in furthering God's kingdom and, like Christ the young prince of glory, walks the royal road of the cross. He lives close to the pattern of God's love for his creation, and shares in his royal power.

The Christian's calling is to live out this life-style of the kingdom in the contemporary world. Within this life-style are the attitudes which are desperately needed if right answers are to be given to social and economic questions, and mankind to come to that fulfilment which is God's purpose for his creation. Yet it is difficult to adopt these attitudes in our daily lives, for they cost us effort, imagination and self-sacrifice. They may also lead us to give generously of our possessions and our wealth in responding to the needs of others. Only if the Spirit of Jesus influences our lives, will such Christ-like attitudes become ours.

7 A Liberating Festival for Mankind

People who are credible

During the summer holidays of 1974, forty thousand young Christians from all over the world met at Taizé, in southern France, for the Council of Youth. They had taken great trouble over some years to prepare themselves for their Council by prayer, reading and discussion, and at the end they wrote a 'Letter to the People of God'. It is a disturbing document which shows that young Christians are deeply concerned about the witness of the churches in the world of our time. Let me quote from their letter:

> Church, what do you say of your future? ... Are you at last going to become a 'universal community of sharing', a community finally reconciled, a place of communion and friendship for the whole of humanity?
>
> Are you going to become the 'people of the beatitudes', having no security other than Christ, a people poor, contemplative, creating peace, bearing joy and a liberating festival for mankind, ready even to be persecuted for justice? [1]

This 'Letter to the People of God' from Taizé puts its finger upon one essential factor in the church's mission. It is not enough for the churches to proclaim the message of hope: their members must live it out in such a way that others can see that the message is true. To quote a recent Anglican report on 'Evangelism and the Mission of the Church': 'the purpose of the church as the community of faith is to make the gospel visible. Its ideals must be incarnate in its members, both individually and corporately. The church *is* the message as well as having it.' [2] Only so will the churches become, in the words of Taizé, 'a place of communion and fellowship for the whole of humanity ... a liberating festival for mankind'.

This is the distinctive contribution which Christians are called to make to the society of which they are members: to contribute to the

70

life of their community those attitudes of trust, commitment and love, which make human life worth living, and lead to the fulfilment of mankind's highest dreams and aspirations. I do not believe that there are specifically Christian solutions to most of our social and economic problems. Their solution often depends upon expert knowledge, painstaking unravelling of issues, and experience. Christians have a part to play in finding these solutions, as colleagues with others in the particular fields in which they have competence: local government, planning, politics or social organization. But over and above these technical contributions, they have certain creative attitudes to offer as they share with others in searching for the answers.

This is what is needed most in our society today: the affirmation of attitudes which make true growth and development possible. We have already referred above to what Gordon Taylor calls 'the paramount question for the next half-century': 'how can we make quality of life, rather than power or profit or gimmickry, the criterion of all our choices?'[3] A similar question was asked by the President of the Royal Town Planning Institute, Ewart Parkinson, in a recent letter to *The Times*.[4] 'For me the central issue is the direction our society wants to take: is it the continuation of the journey we have been making these past hundred years or so, or is there some different direction? ... A new direction would be where we put improvement of quality at the centre of all things instead of the ideal of growth in quantitative terms. This means a fundamental shift in attitude.'

This questioning is expressed by many people in all walks of life, including the politicians. Mr Wedgwood Benn put it this way. 'Just when the breakdown of authoritarianism world wide appears to be reaching a peak, more and more people are searching for guidance. They are, unfortunately, not getting that guidance from their political leaders. There is today a vacuum of the sort of political leadership which analyses, explains, persuades, encourages, discourages and considers expressions of public opinion in order to shape them, by consent, into constructive channels to help create a successful community.'[5]

The Taizé Council of Youth suggested that the People of God, the Church of Christ, are called to be 'people of the beatitudes'; in other words, that they should live out in the communities of which they are members the way of life which Jesus taught. He lived out on earth a truly human life: as a good master-craftsman he invited others to be his 'apprentices' and taught them how to live 'successfully' as the children of God. The secrets of success are those attitudes of confident trust, of responsibility, restraint, renewal and caring which we have discussed in previous chapters. They are the attitudes which the whole human community needs if its members are to realize the full potential of their destiny.

The letter from Taizé, however, came to the churches with a note of disappointment as well as of urgency. 'When are you at last going to become the people of the beatitudes ... a liberating festival for mankind?' they wrote. Their question implies that the churches have not yet become what they are called to be. To put it another way, do the lives of Christians, whether as individuals, or as members of churches, really authenticate the good news which they proclaim to the world?

We proclaim that *God reigns*. But this proclamation raises questions about our own lives and the activities of our congregations. Do our services of worship and fellowship meetings, for example, awaken in others a sense of the presence of the living God? Have we the courage, as Christian communities, to believe that God is leading us on into a future which belongs to him, or do we cling to the traditions of the past in order to protect ourselves against the realities of the present?

We proclaim that *God loves*, but is love the dominant characteristic of our personal lives and the activities of Christian congregations? Are the relationships between people in our congregations, between clergy and laity, between officials and ordinary members, between different groups, clearly ruled by love? Are our ecumenical relationships of such a quality that they help others to believe that it was God who sent Jesus into the world? (John 17.20–21). Do churches pay sufficient attention to the needs of the local communities of which they are part? God in his love wills the well-being of the whole human community and, in praying for his kingdom to come, the churches pledge themselves to seek the fulfilment of God's will in the societies of which they are part. To proclaim that God loves means becoming involved in service to the poor, the outcasts and the underprivileged, and in the struggle for social justice and racial harmony. It means also to support organizations like Christian Aid which have a vital part to play in bridging the gaps between nations and, in particular, between the articulate Western world and the many millions of inarticulate people in Africa and Asia. It means having a personal share in the constant struggle for justice, civil rights and a fairer distribution of the earth's resources.

72

The churches proclaim that *God gives* the resources of his Spirit to enable people to carry out his purposes. This message is heard wherever churches seek those resources and rely upon them, for to use the gifts of the Spirit authenticates a church's message of hope much more than splendid buildings do, or elaborate rituals, an expanding budget or even sound theology and erudite Bible teaching. But the gifts received must be truly those of the Holy Spirit, and touch the whole range of people's lives, responsibilities and actions, in the local community as well as within the churches.

In October 1974, Philip Potter, Secretary General of the World Council of Churches, addressed the Synod of Bishops of the Roman Catholic Church, meeting in Rome. He concluded his speech by quoting the words with which a French bishop had previously addressed the same assembly. 'We lack not so much the words to say to people as credible persons to say the Word.' [6] This is the crucial need of the churches in today's world: to seek for a transparent and recognizable integrity between the great affirmations which they make when proclaiming the good news about God's living involvement with the world, and their corporate life and service. It is by their sincerity that the churches authenticate the good news which they proclaim.

Adjusting the agendas

This is not the place to write at length about the Christian churches and their organizational priorities. There are so many different varieties of church structures among the nations of the world that it is impossible to write a programme which would be appropriate to any but the most local situation. Moreover, as a bishop in an ancient church deeply enmeshed in the law and history of England I know from personal experience how many restraints and limitations can hold a church to old established patterns: I know also the complicated (and often necessary) administrative procedures which hinder change and development. But change is possible and even the most elaborate synodical or organizational machinery is amenable to the will of those who operate it. Moreover it is an accepted truth that the renewal of church life depends upon constant self-reformation in response to the Word of God and the leading of the Holy Spirit. One way to achieve that is to adjust the routine business of a church so that it serves its mission to the world more adequately.

If the churches are to become, in the words of Taizé, 'the people of the beatitudes' and 'a liberating festival for mankind', there must be constant scrutiny of their agendas and structures to see if they are truly relevant to the proclamation of God's good news for the world. Where necessary, they must be adjusted in such a way that the inner life of the church which they serve authenticates the gospel by integrity with it. This is not achieved, however, just by allotting a substantial portion of the time available for council meetings to such topics as 'mission' or 'evangelism', nor is it achieved by seeing that mission boards or departments have a fair slice of the church's cake, whether of finance or manpower. It can only really be achieved by making sure that the business agenda of each church reflects that particular church's commitment to discipleship and to mission.

I suggest that there are three principles which might guide any re-adjustment of a church's agenda and structure in this way.

1. *Integrity of discipleship is more important than correctness of doctrine or ritual.* No Christian would wish to depreciate the importance of sound teaching, regular authority or reverent worship within a church. Such matters, however, are sometimes allowed to usurp the emphasis which the gospels place upon sincere discipleship. It is not those who profess Christ's lordship but those who do the will of his Father who enter the kingdom of Heaven, and the judgment of the Last Day is based upon behaviour towards Christ's needy brethren.[7] Agendas must be planned so that church members may be led and helped to do 'Christ's thing'.

2. *Service of the world is more important than improving church structures.* The whole human community is the object of God's love, for the sake of which Jesus came into the world, suffered and gave his life. He gave all he had to serve its members and to renew them, and he calls his disciples to do the same. If Jesus was 'the man for others', his community also is called to accept a similar role, and to find its purpose in the worship which it offers to God and the ministry it gives to others. This latter ministry includes both loving service to the community, and proclamation within it of the great realities of God. The church's agenda should reflect the needs of the whole society in which its members live.

3. *The universal church is more important than the particular church to which a person or family belongs.* The church is privileged to be the prototype of the world community which is to come. It is a company of men and women from many different nations and races who have this in common, that they follow the Lord Christ and share his Spirit. But the several churches will only play their part in the

attainment of that goal if they respond to each other in trust and love. Only a truly catholic church can serve a world community.

These three principles suggest a number of adjustments which might be made in the agendas of the churches and there are doubtless particular adjustments appropriate for particular churches. Together the churches are called to recover 'visible unity in life and mission',[8] and the attainment of this goal is important if the churches are to be the prototype of God's new humanity. Many of the difficulties which hinder the recovery of visible unity would be overcome if the churches undertook common commitments to basic human projects in terms dictated by the needs of the world rather than by those of the churches and their structures.

Some projects at international level do in fact invite the attention and commitment of the churches. Here are some examples of them.

1. The setting up of an international task-force to assist in major natural disasters. Such a task-force is both necessary and practical in a world which modern communications has made one neighbourhood, and it has the goodwill of many governments, including that of the United Kingdom. The churches already have considerable experience in this field, as well as commitment to it, through Christian Aid, Caritas, and similar organizations.
2. Universal acceptance of a Charter of Human Rights and Responsibilities. This would be an opportunity for the churches to work out the meaning of the gospel in specific social and economic terms, and in company with others.
3. Fairer distribution of the earth's resources and greater equity in the world's commodity markets and monetary system. There are many groups which spend time and effort in these concerns, but the support which they receive from established church organizations is little indeed.
4. Moderation of arms manufacture and of trading in them. With this might well go the imposition of a special tax on their manufacture, the proceeds of which would be used for development purposes in the Third World.

In these and similar projects, the churches would, of course, be involved in discussion with other people. Often they would be in a minority position. But the churches have particular reasons, in the very gospel by which they live, for becoming involved in such projects and they have particular contributions to make. Commitment by the churches to projects such as these in service to the world would be a step forward towards 'visible unity in life and mission'. It would sustain and encourage all those who labour for the building of world community. It would move the churches to minister more directly to the needs of the world, to work in harmony together as the Body of Christ and, by the cost and self-discipline involved, to place discipleship at the top of their agendas.

Across frontiers

Christians are called to authenticate the good news about Christ by the quality of their lives, but they are also called to express it in language and words which those who are not Christians will readily understand. The ambition of every Christian must be to witness to the gospel in as clear and direct a way as Christ did. 'The people all hung upon his words: unlike the doctors of the law, he taught with a note of authority' (Luke 19.48; Mark 1.22).

This is not, however, an easy task to do and in many places Christians find it difficult to express the gospel in ways which appear relevant to their neighbours. They often feel unable to express the good news about God in the words and thought-forms which are used in ordinary, everyday life. New translations of the Bible certainly help but they are not a complete answer, and it sometimes seems as if the Bible view of life is a way of looking at the world which makes little sense for many of our contemporaries. It is as if there were barriers to understanding which Christians find difficult to cross when speaking about their faith.

The apostles themselves, at the beginning of the church's history, were faced with the problem of carrying the gospel across cultural boundaries and the New Testament gives us an idea of how they did this. The gospels show that our Lord's ministry was closely linked with the life and ways of peasant Palestine. It was this which enabled him to make so direct and immediate an impact on his hearers. He drew his parables from the life of the villages in which he worked as a carpenter, and if we had his teaching in Aramaic we would understand better the use which he made of the idioms and rhythms of his native dialect.[9] But, of course, we do not have his words in Aramaic, for the apostles translated them into Greek, almost from the beginning. They did their evangelism in the urban environments of Hellenistic and Roman cities. In doing that they crossed cultural boundaries and we can learn from them. Their achievement was a great one, but we do not always appreciate how great it was. The reason is that, at our distance in time from them, the cultural boundaries between peasant Palestine (especially Gentile Galilee) and Hellenistic cities, appear almost negligible. Distances between nearby objects, however, always diminish when viewed from a distance and I do not think that a first-century observer would have found these cultural barriers insignificant.

In carrying the gospel from peasant Palestine into the provinces of the eastern Roman Empire, the apostles did not only make use of another language. They also developed a second system of images and metaphors, complementary to that of the gospels, to make the good news intelligible to their hearers. Kenneth Cragg calls this 'the trans-language initiative of the New Testament'.[10] We can get an idea of how they did this in several ways. We can, for example, contrast the comparative frequency of key words in the two parts of the New Testament like *kingdom*, *Son of Man*, *disciple* in the gospels and *grace*, *Son of God*, *church* in the epistles. Or we can compare the country parables which Jesus told with St Paul's townsman's images of temples, house-building, conflagrations, race-track and theatre. This task of interpretation was not completed in the age of the apostles: it is the background of Christian history for the first three or four centuries, and the achievement was so thorough and far-reaching that it provided a foundation for European civilization which has lasted for centuries.

The apostles were guided in their work by two principles. First, they expressed the gospel with complete integrity. They were faithful to the good news as they had understood it from the lips of Jesus, and as it had been lived out in his ministry and passion. There is a unity in the New Testament scriptures which is independent of language, and dependent instead upon the reality of the one living God to whom the apostles bear witness.

But secondly, they affirmed the history and achievements of the people among whom they lived and ministered, by using the images, metaphors and ideas which were current coin among them. They did this more thoroughly than interpreters do who simply translate from one language into another. St Paul not only spoke Greek, but on occasions he thought it as well. This is clear from his letters, especially Ephesians and Colossians, and from the speech which Luke attributed to him at Athens.[11] This used many Stoic ideas and it would have been easily understood by the philosophers who listened to him. In St John's gospel, we read the words of an evangelist who had spent many years among the Greek-speaking people at Ephesus:

he was faithful to his memory of Jesus but he told the story in language which would have been intelligible to his friends and in a style appropriate to them.

The churches are called to continue the work of interpretation which the apostles began in carrying the good news from Palestine into the Hellenistic cities of the Roman Empire. They began the task of taking the gospel to the whole world, but its completion depends upon the obedience of each successive generation of Christians. In the complex contemporary world there are several important frontiers which the church is called to cross in carrying the gospel across cultural boundaries. I mention three of them briefly as examples of the work which must be done.

First, the cultures of Asia and Africa, of which other faiths like Islam and Buddhism are integral and determining parts. The Christian task in this context is not to work for the substitution of Western systems of philosophy, but to enter these cultures in and with the Spirit of Christ, just as the apostles and their successors did the philosophy and the ideas of Hellenistic culture. This is a major task for the church in our times and one about which many specialist books have been written.[12]

Secondly, the attitudes towards life and the human adventure which grow out of scientific discovery, and the new perspectives within which modern people think about space and time. Lord Hailsham expressed this particular need for interpretation very forcibly when he wrote a review of the book *Christian Believing* (SPCK 1976) for *The Times*.

> What is needed seems to me to be a reappraisal and reconstruction of Christian thinking by more or less orthodox Christians in terms of contemporary and scientific terminology. We are waiting . . . for a new *doctor angelicus* to elucidate the faith to those who are more familiar with interstellar space and the theory of evolution than fourth century Greek philosophy.[13]

Thirdly, there is need to cross the cultural boundaries which separate the gospel from the modern commercial and industrial world. This is a special concern of St George's House, Windsor, and of Kenneth Adams, until recently its Director of Studies. In an unpublished paper he writes:

> In the sort of agricultural society which the United Kingdom was, up to perhaps the beginning of the nineteenth century, everyone believed unquestionably in the virtue of farming. The symbols and images of good

78

husbandry formed part of the background of the religious beliefs and traditions of the whole society . . . Our industrialized society has failed to break through to an understanding and acceptance of the goodness of the industrial and commercial activities on which it depends for its survival . . . We have no symbols, images and folk tales which assume and assert the underlying goodness of industrialized society.

Christians are called to express the gospel within contexts which are not specifically Christian, like those of other faiths, modern science, or industrial society, just as the apostles were called to do it in the urban cultures of the Hellenistic world. To do this adequately does not ask simply for expert translation of the biblical imagery into the words and idioms of other languages. Such translation can be pedantic and irrelevant. It asks for a much more costly endeavour, that of discovering in these areas the words and metaphors which will express the good news of God's salvation in language which speaks immediately to the hearers without distorting the essentials of the message. It needs creative thinking like that which grew out of St Paul's citizenship in two cultures, or out of the long experience gained by St John in evangelizing the Greeks of Ephesus. In the long run, it can only be done by those who give their whole selves to such an adventure and persevere with it. The church needs many such explorers in order to express the gospel in terms which the whole human family can hear and understand.

A festival for others

The churches are called to *authenticate* the gospel, by life and commitment, and to *articulate* it clearly and directly for the peoples of the world. They are also called to *communicate* it to others. There are, of course, many ways of doing this which it would be tedious to discuss here. Most readers will know of the different methods which the churches use in communicating the gospel to others. They range from the use of radio, television and print to public demonstrations, and they include innumerable acts of personal witness, between friends, at people's doors, and in areas of public meeting. All these methods are valuable and we have probably all been helped by them in one way or another.

The Taizé letter, however, used the phrase 'a liberating festival for mankind' and this goes beyond the techniques of evangelism. This phrase conjures up in my mind the picture of a small mediaeval town celebrating its annual fair. The important people on that day are the players and musicians, the clowns and tumblers, the stall-holders and the criers. By their antics and their enthusiasm, they draw the towns-people into an atmosphere of fun and gaiety, and give them, for a few days at least, a taste of what life might be like if only people could realize their hopes and ideals. On such occasions the usual bye-laws are often suspended, and people act with a freedom and sense of community which they do not usually experience.

Many readers may find it difficult to have a feeling for this kind of festival, for in modern urban society we do not celebrate festivals in this way, and it might help us, therefore, to let our imaginations dwell for a moment on other examples of 'liberating festivals'. Perhaps one or other of them will catch our imagination.

Stories of the circus, written or filmed for children, in the context of small communities where the annual visit of the circus gave a different colour to life for a day or two. (I remember the magic of going with my children to see Professor Wallawalker's Circus, an Indian one, in Amman, the capital of Jordan. Its joyous influence on all five of us lasted for days.)

Carnival days in seaside towns in Britain: no one who has shared in the work of decorating a float, and then had the excitement of riding on it through beflagged streets and crowds of townsfolk, will forget the commitment as well as the fun of such occasions.

Festivals of saints or flowers in Spain or Portugal, or in South America.

Much the same feeling of excitement and well-being pervades Muslim cities during the 'Id al-Adha, or at the end of Ramadan, or on the Mulid Festival (the Prophet's Birthday). The streets are gaily lit, food is given liberally to the poor, people are in their best clothes, and during the space of two or three days, neighbours and friends visit each other all across the city.

We must have occasions like these in our minds when we try to interpret the Taizé phrase, 'a liberating festival for mankind'. We should link it also with the instances in the gospels where our Lord likened the kingdom of God to a marriage-feast or a party.[14] We should link it also with the holy communion, which is itself a fore-taste of the heavenly banquet (see above, page 55). Christians are called to live out in the world the realities of God's sovereignty; the joyous confidence which grows out of experiencing his grace, the capacity for renewal and triumph which comes from the victory of our Lord, the inner resources of God's Spirit which refresh, purify and inspire human lives. By living thus as God intended people to do, Christians are signs and symbols for others of their liberation and fulfilment. They bring into the life of the whole community those attitudes of trust and hope, of love, of peace and joy, which can change the whole quality of human society. Thus they become the salt which Christ called them to be, purifying and giving flavour to the whole mix.

At the beginning of this book, I stated that my aim was to help readers understand what mission is and to see it as an integral part of God's activity within the human community. In the previous chapters I have tried to show how God is involved in the whole on-going development of the human community, and how he is working for its fulfilment both here and now, and also beyond space and time. In working towards that fulfilment, he gives himself to the world graciously and generously: he overcame evil by bearing its pain and hurt in the person of our Lord, and he makes that same victory a reality in the lives of those who allow him to do so: he gives them also the resources of his Spirit. All this ceaseless, loving activity is the mission of God. It is the Christian's privilege to live by those realities, in the fellowship of the church, and to make them real and intelligible for others. To live like that is to have a personal share in the mission of God, and to liberate others to share in his festival.

Two years after the Council of Youth, the *Letter from Taizé* asked this question:

Certain that a small number of women and men, spread across the face of the earth, striving to reconcile in themselves struggle and contemplation, can change the course of history and reinvent the world:

Because of the risen Christ, are you going to risk your life day after day, constantly setting out anew, never discouraged because loved with Eternity's love?

With the whole of God's people, will you open up paths of hope for all the human family? [15]

The human adventure is one of hope because tomorrow belongs to God. To share that hope with others is to share in the mission of God.

Postscript: Think Big – Act Small

Sir Bernard Lovell began his Presidential Address to the British Association, to which I have already referred above (page 40), by quoting from Thomas Carlyle's *Sartor Resartus*. 'What is Man, who sees and fashions for himself a Universe, with starry spaces and long thousands of years . . . as it were, swathed in and inextricably over-shrouded; yet it is sky-woven and worthy of a God? Stands he not thereby in the centre of Immensities, in the complex of Eternities?'

This is man's high dignity, to measure the immensities of the universe in which he lives, to probe the great distances of the heavens, to look back down the long corridors of geological time and to distinguish the great complexities in the species of living creatures, or in the materials of the natural universe. His science is an immense achievement, made possible by the long labours of generations of scientists, but open to every school child. To open doors on to this great wealth of knowledge is to be rich indeed.

To possess this knowledge about the natural universe, however, is not enough. There are other immensities which crowd in upon men and women, and threaten or ennoble human existence: the great power which evil has to destroy human communities, the immense power of love and self-sacrifice to redeem situations and to transform them, and the capacity to dream and to hope for new patterns of existence and fulfilment. Man is, on the one hand, a creature living out his small time-bound life within the conditions enforced by his natural environment: on the other hand, he is called by God's eternal purpose and, through worship, enters into a relationship with him which has no ending. He is both a creature, one of earth's innumer-able tenants, and also a child of God, touched by eternity. To live aright, to be aware of himself and his destiny, man needs more than scientific understanding: he needs a world-view which integrates his scientific understanding with a vision of the eternal purpose for which mankind was created, and which has been inherent in all the processes of evolution.

Such a vision is urgently needed in our contemporary world where the human community has reached a turning-point in its growth and development. As we saw in the first chapter, the rate of change is so great and the new powers which lie within men's grasp so enormous that they produce pressures and tensions which threaten to overwhelm us. Yet together with these pressures and tensions there has also come the possibility of a leap forward towards a community which will span the world and bring the fragmented achievements of all the nations to a harmonious fulfilment. Mankind needs the inspiration of a vision which matches the opportunities and dangers of this particular stage in world history, and new qualities of the spirit by which to respond to it.

Those who are Christians dare to believe that in walking along the road of life as disciples of the Lord Jesus they are given such a vision and the resources to achieve it.

They learn in the perplexities and uncertainties of life to trust in God as King and Father;

They discover the immense power of God to renew and recreate, even in the face of defeat and despair;

They learn to think of others as brothers and sisters who have a claim upon them, and to act with responsibility and restraint;

They draw on resources of spiritual power and are open to the influence of the divine Spirit;

They are given a vision of Jerusalem, the city of God, in which human history finds fulfilment;

They are helped to be open towards truth and to affirm the gracious activity of God throughout his whole universe.

This world-view, however, is not a philosophy given through book-learning nor is it a body of truth which can be taught simply by classes or through sermons. It is not a view gained from a balcony overlooking the highway, but, in the words of John Mackay to which we referred earlier (page 27), on the road of life itself. It becomes part of our lives as we are apprenticed to Christ the master-craftsman and are inspired by his Spirit.

It would be foolish to pretend that all who name the name of Christ or worship in Christian churches walk the road in this way: and there are many others who are companions of Christ who would not use his name. Moreover, there are valuable contributions to the human adventure which come from other communities and other faiths. But when the church has been true to itself and to its Lord it has given the gift of this vision to those who share in its fellowship. It is a gift to share with the nations. Christians who know it and Christians who share it are the salt which could purify and save the world.

In December 1975, the BBC presented a short documentary on the work of the churches in Luton. Among others, an industrial chaplain was shown doing his rounds in a car factory. Asked about his ministry, he said that he and his colleagues were learning to 'think big and act small'. This is the Christian's calling: to worship the living God, and, 'thinking big', to rejoice at all he sees of God's activity in the natural universe, in the human community, and in his own life: to live confidently and courageously as a citizen of God's Jerusalem: but also, 'acting small', to care for his neighbour in terms of his neighbour's need, and to give of his best in the particular circumstances where he or she is called or compelled to live: to be husband, wife, parent, employer or employee in the particular circumstances of his or her personal situation. This was the way of Christ, the Eternal Son of God who was content to be the carpenter of Nazareth, the prophet of Galilee, and one of three on Calvary's hill. In the end, it is the dignity and glory of every human person.

Notes

Chapter 1. The Ascent of Man (pp. 1–10)

1. Alister Hardy, *The Living Stream*, Collins 1965, p. 30.
2. Pierre Teilhard de Chardin, *The Phenomenon of Man*, Collins 1959; Fontana 1965, p. 134.
3. Lutterworth Press 1973.
4. Quoted by André Dumas in 'Unity of Mankind – Unity of the Church', *Study Encounter*, WCC, Vol. X, No. 2, 1974, p. 11.
5. No. 7, February 1975, pp. 41–2.

Chapter 2. We Have a Dream (pp. 11–22)

1. Theodosius Dobzhansky, *The Biology of Ultimate Concern*, Fontana 1967, p. 108.
2. Pan Books, 2nd ed. 1973.
3. Op. cit., pp. 248–9.
4. Martin Luther King, *Marching to Freedom*, New American Library 1967, pp. 107, 121.
5. Martin Luther King, *Chaos or Community?*, Penguin 1969, p. 181.
6. André Dumas, art. cit., p. 18.
7. Pierre Teilhard de Chardin, *Building the Earth*, Geoffrey Chapman 1965.
8. Mehajlo Mesarovic and Eduard Pestel, *Mankind at the Turning Point*, Hutchinson 1975.
9. *The Limits to Growth*, Earth Island Ltd 1972.
10. Op. cit., pp. 1–9.
11. See Gen. 11.1–9: 12.1–4.
12. E.g. Isa. 1.26; Micah 4.1–8; Heb. 11.10, 13–16: 12.22–3.
13. Phil. 2.20; John 18.36.
14. See John Stott, *The Lausanne Covenant*, World Wide Publications, Minneapolis 1975, pp. 20, 25, 30, 36, 56.
15. Pierre Teilhard de Chardin, *Hymn of the Universe*, Collins 1965; Fontana 1970, Pensée 37.

16. Reported in *The Times*, 27 May 1974.

17. *Communion*, Taizé Community, No. 7, February 1975, pp. 2, 48.

Chapter 3. *Salt to the World* (*pp. 23–32*)

1. See e.g. Dan. 12.1–4.

2. Mark 1.14–15; Luke 4.18, 23: 19.38, 44: 17.21 (NEBm): 11.20.

3. Luke 22.28–9; Acts 2.33: 8.12: 20.24.

4. Luke 17.24: 21.27, 36; Matt. 25.31–46. See Joachim Jeremias, *New Testament Theology*, Vol. 1, SCM Press 1971, pp. 272–6.

5. Sister Madeleine OSA, *Solitary Refinement*, SCM Press 1972, pp. 37–8.

6. Jeremias, op. cit., p. 311.

7. 'The time has come; the kingdom of God is upon you; repent and believe the Gospel' (Mark 1.15).

8. *The Limits to Growth*, p. 195.

9. Gordon Rattray Taylor, *Rethink*, Penguin 1974, ch. 1, esp. pp. 20, 347.

10. John Mackay, *A Preface to Christian Theology*, James Nisbet 1942.

11. Luke 5.27–8: 9.23: 18.22; John 1.44; Acts 9.2: 18.25–6: 19.9.

12. Trevor Beeson, *Discretion and Valour*, Fontana 1974.

13. David Barrett, 'AD 2000: 350 million Christians in Africa', *International Review of Missions*, Vol. LIX, January 1970, p. 51.

14. Mark 2.15–17: 1.35–9: 10.32–4.

15. Matt. 5.13, 14; Mark 10.35–45; John 13.1–17.

16. Matt. 28.19–20; Mark 16.16; Acts 1.8.

Chapter 4. *Amazing Grace* (*pp. 33–45*)

1. *al-Ikhlas*, sura 112.

2. OUP 1965.

3. W. Schmidt, *The Origin and Growth of Religion*, 1931, p. 6.

4. J. Bronowski, *The Ascent of Man*, BBC Publications 1973, p. 353.

5. Amos 4.13.

6. From the *Bhagavad-gita*, tr. R. C. Zaehner, OUP 1969, pp. 85–6.

7. *Readings from the Mystics of Islam*, tr. Margaret Smith, Luzac 1950, p. 60.

8. H. Gravrand, *Meeting the African Religions*, Ancora, Rome 1968, p. 173.

9. See Luke 15.

10. T. W. Manson, *The Sayings of Jesus*, SCM Press 1949, p. 345.

11. Jeremias, op. cit., p. 178.

12. F. D. Coggan, *The Prayers of the New Testament*, Hodder 1967, pp. 117–18.

13. Gal. 2.20; 11 Cor. 8.9.

14. Sir Bernard Lovell, OBE, FRS, 'In the Centre of Immensities', *The Advancement of Science*, No. 1, 29 August 1975.

15. See, e.g., David Dineley, *Earth's Voyage Through Time*, Paladin 1975, pp. 309, 329.

16. The simplest form of the prayer is in Luke 11.2–4, and a variant of it in Matt. 6.9–13.

17. Mark 14.36; Luke 23.46. The Aramaic word is used even in Gal. 4.6 and Rom. 8.15, which were letters written to Greek-speaking congregations.

18. Luke 11.1–4. I have taken the text of the Lord's prayer from the Anglican Series 3 Service of Holy Communion.

19. Much of the story is told in Oliver Allison, *Through Fire and Water*, CMS 1976.

20. *The Trial of Beyers Naudé*, Search Press 1975, pp. 59–60.

Chapter 5. Young Prince of Glory (*pp. 46–59*)

1. I Cor. 2.1–2; Gal. 3.1.

2. John 13.21; see also 12.27.

3. Mark 15.34; Luke 23.46.

4. Mark 2.18–20: 8.27–33.

5. The passages referred to are principally the four 'Songs of the Servant' which are found in Isa. 42.1–9: 49.1–7: 50.4–11: 52.13–53.12.

6. Almost every standard work of Christian theology includes a main section on the passion narrative, and the doctrine of the atonement.

7. See James Macnair, *Livingstone' Travels*, Dent 1954, pp. 378–9.

8. See Rev. 5.6. 'The Lamb' is here a title for Christ, and 'the marks of slaughter' interprets his death in sacrificial terms.

9. Qur'an 40.7 and 113–114.

10. Q. 6.125.

11. Q. 4.155–62.

12. The Qur'anic passages about the passion of Jesus are discussed in my book *The Cross of the Messiah*, SPCK 1967.

13. From Lynn de Silva, 'Buddhism' in *A Guide to Religions*, ed. David Brown, SPCK 1975, pp. 126–7.

14. Op. cit., p. 129.

15. Rev. 21.27; see also ch. 2 above.

16. II Cor. 5.17 (NEBm); James 1.18; Rev. 14.4.

17. Rom. 8.29: 5.12–21; I Cor. 15.45–9.

18. See references in ch. 3, n. 11.

19. The principal passages are Eph. 4.17–6.20; Col. 3.1–4.6; I Peter 2.11–3.18. An interesting discussion of the whole subject will be found in E. G. Selwyn, *The First Epistle of St Peter*, Macmillan 1949, Essay II.

20. Q. 2.30–31.

21. An article in *Commonwealth*, Royal Commonwealth Society, March 1975.

22. Acts 20.35; Luke 9.58.

23. SCM Press 1975.

Chapter 6. Resources of Power (pp. 60–69)

1. See, e.g., David Dineley, *Earth's Voyage Through Time*, Paladin 1975.
2. John 20.19–23 and Acts 2.1–4; Rom. 8.9.
3. Joel 2.28–9; Eph. 2.22; I Cor. 6.19.
4. Gen. 1.2; Ex. 35.30–36.1; II Sam. 23.1–2; I Sam. 11.1–11; Isa. 11.1–9; Num. 24.1–9; Ezek. 11.18, 24.
5. See I Cor. 12–14.
6. Acts 6.5–10: 8.26–40: 13.1–3: 16.6–10: 1.8.
7. Léon-Joseph, Cardinal Suenens, *A New Pentecost?*, Darton, Longman & Todd 1975, p. 227.
8. As reported in the *Church Times*, 12 September 1975.

Chapter 7. A Liberating Festival for Mankind (pp. 70–81)

1. 'Letter to the People of God', Taizé Community, 1 September 1974.
2. General Synod document GS 222, CIO 1974, p. 10.
3. See above, p. 26.
4. 7 January 1976.
5. From a speech made in Germany, reported in *The Times*, 12 April 1972.
6. From 'A Monthly Letter about Evangelism', WCC, No. 1, January 1975.
7. Matt. 7.21–3: 25.31–46.
8. The first proposition of the Churches Unity Commission (England 1976) states: 'We reaffirm our belief that the visible unity in life and mission of all Christ's people is the will of God.'
9. Cf. Jeremias, op. cit., ch. 1.
10. See his *Christianity in World Perspective*, Lutterworth Press 1968, esp. ch. 2.
11. St Paul's speech is found in Acts 17.22–34. I have explored this theme in a CMS sermon, January 1976, 'Doorways and Doorsteps', published by the Highway Press.
12. See, e.g., my *A Guide to Religions*, SPCK 1975, and its bibliography.
13. 21 February 1976.
14. E.g. Mark 2.18–20; Luke 13.29: 14.15–24: 15.22–4.
15. *Letter from Taizé*, No. 26, May 1976.